AIR CAMPAIGN

CENTRAL PACIFIC 1943–45

Seventh Air Force's island-hopping war

BRIAN LANE HERDER | ILLUSTRATED BY GARETH HECTOR

OSPREY PUBLISHING
Bloomsbury Publishing Plc
Kemp House, Chawley Park, Cumnor Hill, Oxford OX2 9PH, UK
Bloomsbury Publishing Ireland Limited,
29 Earlsfort Terrace, Dublin 2, D02 AY28, Ireland
1385 Broadway, 5th Floor, New York, NY 10018, USA
E-mail: info@ospreypublishing.com
www.ospreypublishing.com

OSPREY is a trademark of Osprey Publishing Ltd

First published in Great Britain in 2025

© Osprey Publishing Ltd, 2025

All rights reserved. No part of this publication may be: i) reproduced or transmitted in any form, electronic or mechanical, including photocopying, recording or by means of any information storage or retrieval system without prior permission in writing from the publishers; or ii) used or reproduced in any way for the training, development or operation of artificial intelligence (AI) technologies, including generative AI technologies. The rights holders expressly reserve this publication from the text and data mining exception as per Article 4(3) of the Digital Single Market Directive (EU) 2019/790.

A catalog record for this book is available from the British Library.

ISBN: PB 9781472864871; eBook 9781472864888; ePDF 9781472864857; XML 9781472864864

25 26 27 28 29 10 9 8 7 6 5 4 3 2 1

Maps and diagrams by www.bounford.com
3D BEVs by Paul Kime
Index by Richard Munro
Typeset by Ditech Process Solutions Private Limited
Printed by Repro India Ltd.

Title page: See caption on p. 20.

Osprey Publishing supports the Woodland Trust, the UK's leading woodland conservation charity.

To find out more about our authors and books, visit www.ospreypublishing.com. Here you will find extracts, author interviews, details of forthcoming events and the option to sign up for our newsletter.

For product safety-related questions, contact productsafety@bloomsbury.com

AIR CAMPAIGN

CONTENTS

INTRODUCTION	4
CHRONOLOGY	8
ATTACKER'S CAPABILITIES	11
DEFENDER'S CAPABILITIES	26
CAMPAIGN OBJECTIVES	31
THE CAMPAIGN	35
AFTERMATH AND ANALYSIS	92
SELECT BIBLIOGRAPHY	94
INDEX	95

INTRODUCTION

Three P-47N Thunderbolts flying in formation, circa 1945. The P-47N was specifically developed for Very Long Range escort missions against Japan. Nevertheless, the role remains best remembered through the P-51D VLR groups stationed at Iwo Jima. (Public Domain)

The Pacific War has often been described as a war to seize locations from which to project airpower. Nowhere was this truer than in the 1943–45 Central Pacific campaign, where islands and atolls were so small and so far apart that they almost always had to be taken by direct physical assault onto heavily-defended beaches. The high coordination of combined arms and joint forces required to successfully conquer fortified Central Pacific islands demanded a great level of interservice coordination. The USAAF's contribution to this campaign was the US Seventh Air Force. Unfortunately, its contributions to final Pacific victory have always been lost in the glare of its two giant and famous operating partners: the US Navy's Fast Carrier Task Force and the Twentieth Air Force's B-29s.

The US Seventh Air Force was originally known as the Hawaiian Air Force, which its members inevitably nicknamed the "Pineapple Air Force." Despite getting decimated at Pearl Harbor, the USAAF ultimately assigned the Seventh responsibility for the new Central Pacific Area of operations which (except for Midway) was largely very quiet. But when the US Navy began its Central Pacific counteroffensive in late 1943, the Seventh Air Force automatically became the USAAF's primary contribution to the theater. Operations transformed from training services to combat operations.

The Seventh Air Force participated in all the major 1943–45 Central Pacific island campaigns (Gilberts, Marshalls, Marianas, Iwo Jima, Okinawa) as air support for the invasions. Following each conquest, a Seventh Air Force detachment was assigned to the occupied island as the island's organic air defense, and also to keep the surrounding Japanese-occupied islands neutralized by bombing them on a near daily basis. After providing a major part of the air support and fighter defense during the Iwo Jima and Okinawa battles, P-51s and P-47s of the Seventh Air Force's VII Fighter Command were assigned to escort the B-29s to Japan. Eventually, the USAAF decided escorting B-29s was unnecessary, and the P-51s and P-47s spent the last few months of the war conducting low-level bombing and strafing raids against Home Islands assets in preparation for Operation *Olympic*.

Despite its relatively small size compared to other numbered air forces, the Seventh deployed the widest array of aircraft types, perhaps an indicator of its relatively low priority until late in the war. Eleven different aircraft types were operated by the Seventh Air Force during the 1943–45 Central Pacific campaign. These were the B-24, B-25, A-24, A-26, P-38, P-39, P-40, P-47, P-51, P-61, and P-70. At times, the Seventh wielded operational control over naval or marine air units equipped with naval aircraft types, such as the FG Corsair and F6F Hellcat at Okinawa.

Even for the Pacific War, the command relationship of the USAAF Seventh Air Force was unusually complex. There were several interrelated reasons for this. First, the Seventh Air Force's geographic domain was the Central Pacific, a region dominated by vast ocean interrupted only by the smallest islands often thousands of miles apart. Secondly, this oceanic theater was firmly dominated by US Navy command as part of the Pacific Ocean Areas. Thirdly, the nature of Central Pacific island-hopping operations meant all four services (USAAF, USN, US Army, and USMC) would be heavily intermixed in joint commands to a degree not seen in any other wartime theater. Therefore, while this title is primarily concerned with the USAAF Seventh Air Force, it will also examine as necessary USN, USMC, and US Army contingents that fought alongside the Seventh Air Force within the same joint task forces.

The Seventh Air Force was established in November 1940 as the Hawaiian Air Force. A USAAF-wide reorganization caused all named air forces to be re-designated by Arabic digits before finally being spelled out. The result was the "7" prominently featured in the wartime patch of the Seventh Air Force. (Public Domain)

Prelude: 1941–42

No numbered US air force entered the war saddled with such ignominy as did the Seventh Air Force.

On November 1, 1940, the US Army Air Corps established the Hawaiian Air Force, comprising the 18th Bombardment Wing of B-10 Martins at Hickam Field and the 14th Pursuit Wing of P-26 Peashooters at Wheeler Field. The United States' existing air corridor from Hawaii to the Philippines ran through Wake and Guam, which were dangerously close to Japanese airbases in the Marshalls and Marianas. With relations deteriorating, in August 1941 the USAAF began developing a new Hawaii–Australia air route safer from Japanese interference, establishing new airfields on Christmas, Canton, Samoa, Fiji, and New Caledonia.

On December 7, 1941, six Japanese fleet carriers launched 343 sorties against the US base at Pearl Harbor. Although the Japanese achieved complete surprise, 14 Hawaiian Air Force pilots made it aloft during the attack. Aerial losses were two P-40s on takeoff, one P-36 in a dogfight, and one P-36 to friendly anti-aircraft fire. In turn, they shot down 11 Japanese attackers.

Pearl Harbor was nevertheless a staggering defeat for the Hawaiian Air Force, which had utterly failed in its only mission and been incapacitated in the process. Of its 231 aircraft early on December 7, 1941, only 79 survived the attack in a usable state. Sixty-four planes had been destroyed, with many more damaged. Hawaiian Air Force casualties were 206 killed or missing and 336 wounded. Of these, 158 were killed or missing and 274 wounded at Hickam Field.

Pearl Harbor demanded a total shakeup of the USAAF, especially in Hawaii. In January 1942, an Osage Native American, Clarence L. Tinker, was promoted to major-general and commander of the Hawaiian Air Force. Then on February 5, 1942, the Hawaiian Air Force was re-designated the 7th Air Force, which was re-styled as the Seventh Air Force

INTRODUCTION

Boeing B-17 Flying Fortresses make a flyby of Hickam Field in summer 1941. The B-17 served the VII Bomber Command during its early days. By far the most important performance factor in the Central Pacific theater was range, and the B-17's range fell short of the B-24s. In late 1942 the USAAF began phasing the B-17 out of the Pacific theater. By late 1942 the B-17 had been entirely replaced in the VII Bomber Command's heavy bomber role by the longer-legged B-24 Liberator. (Public Domain)

on September 18, 1942.[1] The 18th Bombardment Wing and 14th Pursuit Wing were re-designated the VII Bomber Command and VII Fighter Command, respectively. The VII Base Command assumed responsibility for various base and service functions, along with the Hawaiian Air Depot.

After Pearl Harbor the shattered Seventh Air Force was tasked with rebuilding itself and guarding against any future Japanese attack in the Central Pacific. Through May 1942 its mission was entirely defensive. For the Seventh Air Force this meant overwater search flights, with forces always prepared to strike any observed contact. Daily missions were flown covering the Hawaiian Islands over an 800-mile radius. Because patrol flights flew zigzag patterns instead of straight out and straight back, this meant round-trip flights of more than 1,800 miles.

The search missions helped train aircrews in overwater flights, resulting in the navigator becoming the key member of a bomber crew. For additional training, the Seventh Air Force started making round-trip flights to Johnston Island, a small isolated atoll over 750 miles southwest of Oahu. These missions were timed so that the bombers would fly to Johnston in daylight and fly back at night, ensuring full round-the-clock flying and navigating skills.

However, in late May 1942, naval intelligence predicted an impending major attack against Midway. The Seventh Air Force flew in 17 B-17s and four B-26s to defend the atoll. Between June 3 and June 5, the Midway-based B-17s made 16 separate attacks against the Japanese fleet in 55 sorties. On June 4, four B-26s, jury-rigged with Mark 13 torpedoes, made a daring low-level attack against the main Japanese carrier force. A fatally damaged B-26 attempted a suicide dive against the wildly maneuvering *Akagi*, only just missing the carrier by yards.

Strictly speaking, the Seventh Air Force's material contribution to Midway was inconsequential, as it inflicted no damage to Japanese warships. However, the incessant and aggressive attacks by Seventh Air Force units unnerved and frustrated the Japanese, indirectly contributing to the overwhelmingly successful USN dive-bomber strike on June 4.

1 For simplicity, the 7th Air Force will be referred to hereafter as the Seventh Air Force.

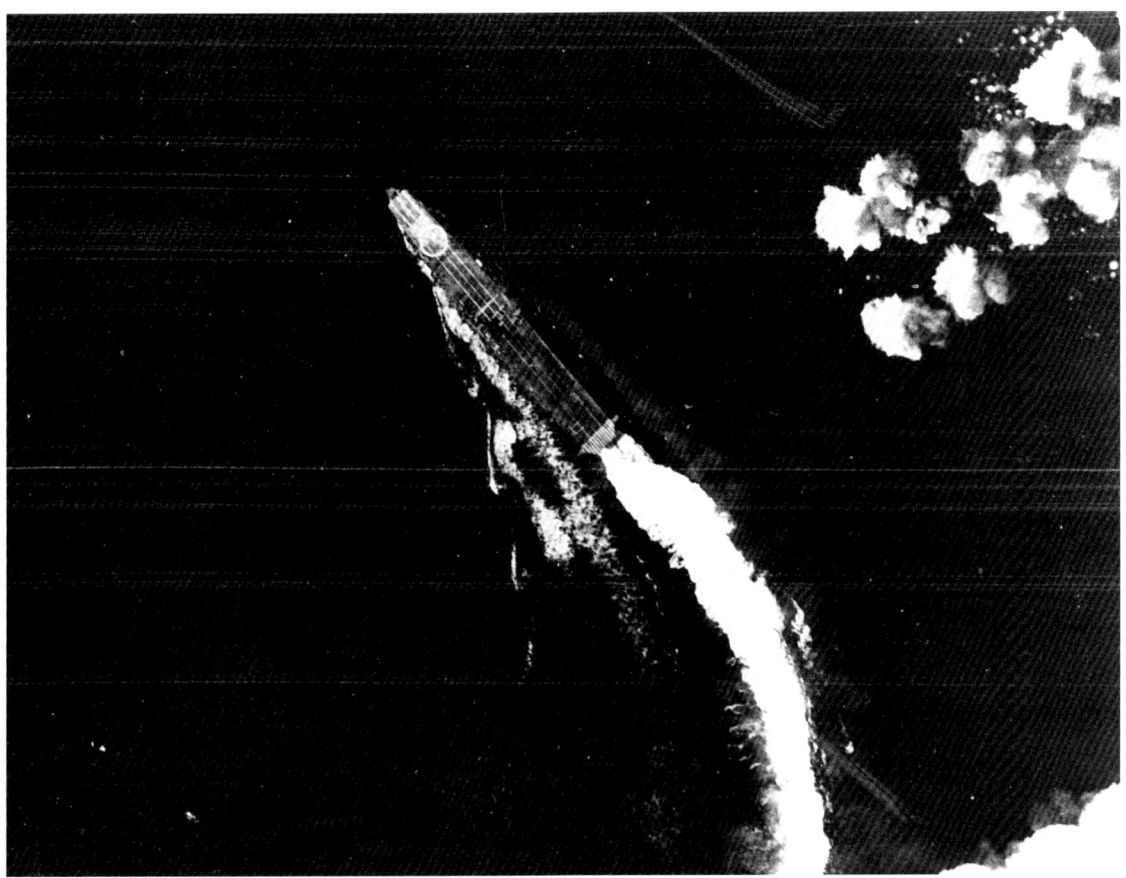

The Japanese aircraft carrier *Hiryu* successfully evades the bombs of a Seventh Air Force B-17E off Midway around 0800hrs on the morning of June 4, 1942. Virtually all photographs of the Japanese carriers from June 4 were taken by the Seventh Air Force, not the USN carrier planes. (Public Domain)

The Seventh Air Force however suffered heavy casualties during the battle. Among these were on June 6, when Tinker led a nighttime attack by four LB-30s (Lend-Lease B-24 versions) to Wake hoping to find the fleeing Japanese fleet. Tinker's LB-30 got lost and crashed in the ocean, killing the Seventh Air Force commander. Hawaii-based B-17s would attack Wake in July 1942 and again in December 1942. These raids were virtually the only action for the rest of the year.

In early 1943 Seventh Air Force B-24s struck Japanese bases at Nauru and Tarawa in the Gilberts, but it was not until the fall of 1943 that construction of advance bases far out into the Central Pacific allowed the Seventh Air Force to deploy deep into the Central Pacific and begin planning systematic strike operations against the Japanese-occupied Gilberts.

CHRONOLOGY

1940
November 1 Hawaiian Air Force established at Fort Shafter, Hawaii Territory.

1941
December 7 Japanese surprise attack against Pearl Harbor heavily damages the Hawaiian Air Force.

1942
February 5 Hawaiian Air Force re-designated 7th Air Force. The 18th Bombardment Wing is reorganized as VII Bomber Command. The 5th Pursuit Wing is reorganized as VII Fighter Command. The VII Base Command assumes responsibility for various base and service functions, along with the Hawaiian Air Depot.

June 4–6 7th Air Force units suffer heavy casualties aggressively attacking the Japanese fleet off Midway the morning of June 4. Although 7th Air Force bombers inflict zero direct damage against any Japanese warships, their incessant attacks indirectly contribute to the overwhelmingly successful USN dive-bombing strike the morning of June 4.

September 18 7th Air Force re-designated Seventh Air Force.

1943
November 20 Operation *Galvanic* D-Day as Central Pacific Force lands on Tarawa and Makin.

November 24 Tarawa and Makin secured; respective garrison groups arrive and begin building airfields at both islands.

December Seventh Air Force begins strikes on Marshalls from its new Gilberts bases.

1944
February 1 Operation *Flintlock* D-Day as US forces land at Kwajalein.

February 14 Hoover's command re-designated Commander, Central Pacific Forward Area.

March 14 The Seventh Air Force raids Truk for the first time.

May 1 Hale assumes command of Task Force 59 (Commander, Air, Forward), remaining under Hoover's command. Brigadier-General Robert W. Douglas, Jr assumes command of the Seventh Air Force in place of Hale.

June 15 Operation *Forager* D-Day as US ground forces land at Saipan.

June 22 First Seventh Air Force P-47s land at Saipan and immediately begin close air support missions.

August 1 US Seventh Air Force subordinated to the newly-activated Army Air Forces, Pacific Ocean Areas (AAFPOA) command.

Vice Admiral John H. Hoover in 1942. Hoover, a US naval aviator, was the intermediary commander between Seventh Air Force and CINCPOA. Hoover's acerbic personality inspired the sardonic nickname "Genial John." The highest-ranking US naval aviator, Vice Admiral John H. Towers, described Hoover as: "An enigma. Physically fit. A positive character. Not popular. Standoffish. Lack of close relationship between him and his staff…" (Public Domain)

December 8 US Seventh Air Force and US naval forces launch the first combined arms bombardment of Iwo Jima airfields.

1945

February 16 Operation *Detachment* (invasion of Iwo Jima) commences with three days of pre-invasion air-sea bombardment by US forces, including the Seventh Air Force.

February 19 US V Amphibious Corps begins initial D-Day landings on Iwo Jima.

March 6 The 15th Fighter Group's 47th Fighter Squadron and 548th Night Fighter Squadron depart Saipan and land at Iwo Jima's South Field, the first echelon in an eventual total transfer of the 15th, 21st, and 506th Fighter Groups from the Marianas to Iwo Jima.

March 7 The 15th Fighter Group and 548th Night Fighter Squadron begin round-the-clock CAPs (Combat Air Patrols) over Iwo Jima.

March 10 15th Fighter Group P-51s begin dawn-till-dusk on-call CAS (Close Air Support) missions over Iwo Jima.

March 10–11 First major nighttime incendiary raid by XXI Bomber Command B-29s against the Home Islands, signaling an eventual shift in tactics that will transform VII Fighter Command VLR missions from planned bomber escort to offensive sweeps against Home Islands surface targets.

March 11 Colonel Jim Beckwith leads 17 Iwo Jima-based P-51 Mustangs of the 47th Fighter Squadron in a bombing raid against Chichi Jima, the first in near-daily P-51 strikes against Bonin Islands airfields.

March 14 VII Fighter Command P-51s fly last CAS mission against Iwo Jima defenders.

March 25 Initial air-sea pre-invasion bombardment commences for Operation *Iceberg*, the planned US amphibious invasion of Okinawa.

March 26 Some 350 Japanese troops launch early-morning last-ditch banzai charge against Iwo Jima's US-occupied Central Field and are repulsed by Seventh Air Force personnel.

March 29 Iwo Jima-based P-61s begin nightly heckler missions against Bonin Islands airfields.

The US Fast Carrier Task Force at Ulithi, December 8, 1944. From front to back: USS *Wasp* (CV-18), USS *Yorktown* (CV-10), USS *Hornet* (CV-12), USS *Hancock* (CV-19) and USS *Ticonderoga* (CV-14). The fast carriers provided the bulk of airpower during the initial stages of any Central Pacific invasion. Because they were highly vulnerable to counterattack, they needed land-based aircraft to take over as soon as possible. (NHHC 80-G-294131)

April 1 L-Day for Operation *Iceberg* – US Tenth Army begins initial landings on Okinawa, capturing Kadena and Yontan airfields within a few hours.

April 7 P-51s of the Iwo Jima-based 15th and 21st Fighter Groups mount the first VLR mission to the Home Islands, escorting a B-29 raid against Tokyo.

April 16–21 US 77th Infantry Division assaults and captures island of Ie Shima off the coast of Okinawa; Ie Shima will soon become a major VII Fighter Command base.

May 11 The XXX Fighter Group (111 P-47N Thunderbolts) begins arriving at Ie Shima.

July 14 US Seventh Air Force officially transferred to US Far East Air Forces (FEAF).

July 16 US Twentieth Air Force reorganized to include VII Fighter Command alongside XXI Bomber Command.

July 29–August 1 Seventh Air Force launches strategic bombing campaign against Nagasaki.

August 4 Last Japanese night bomber raid against Iwo Jima.

August 14 Japanese government surrenders.

ATTACKER'S CAPABILITIES
Gaining control of the islands

US Central Pacific tactics were to seize island air and sea bases from the Japanese and then secure them from counterattack. For the Seventh Air Force this would be accomplished by smothering all Japanese airfields within range. Additionally, Seventh Air Force would execute ground support sorties in conjunction with the Central Pacific landings. Strategic bombing was a distant second priority for most of the 1943–45 campaign, with the Seventh's only true strategic bombing campaign waged against steel and shipbuilding plants in Nagasaki between July 29 and August 1, 1945.

The Bell P-39 Airacobra was one of two standard day fighters employed by the Seventh Air Force at the beginning of the 1943–45 Central Pacific drive. This Airacobra, a P-39Q, is seen here in 1940. The P-39, P-40, and P-38 were all derived from the same US Army Air Corps circular proposal in February 1937. (Public Domain)

Commands

On March 24, 1942, the Anglo-American Combined Chiefs of Staff (CCS) designated the Pacific Ocean to be an American area of strategic responsibility. On March 30, the US Joint Chiefs of Staff (JCS) divided the Pacific Ocean into three areas: the Pacific Ocean Areas (POA), the South-West Pacific Area (SWPA), and the South-East Pacific Area (SEPA). The POA encompassed the majority of the Pacific Ocean. However, mainland Asia, the Philippines, the Netherlands East Indies, Australia, New Guinea, and the western Solomon Islands fell under the South-West Pacific Area. Command of the South-West Pacific Area was given to General Douglas MacArthur.

The JCS appointed Admiral Chester Nimitz as commander-in-chief of the Pacific Ocean Areas (CINCPOA), effective May 8, 1942. Nimitz was thus assigned operational control of all Allied air, land, and sea forces in the POA, essentially giving the US Navy operational control of the theater. The JCS additionally divided the POA into three separate areas: the North Pacific Area, the Central Pacific Area, and the South Pacific Area. This formally put all forces in the North Pacific, Central Pacific, and South Pacific Areas under USN operational command. This included the USAAF's Hawaii-based Seventh Air Force.

ATTACKER'S CAPABILITIES

Fleet Admiral Chester Nimitz seen immediately postwar as the USN's new Chief of Naval Operations. Nimitz wore two "hats" in the Pacific, as he was commander-in-chief of both the US Pacific Fleet (CINCPAC), and also commander-in-chief of the Pacific Ocean Areas (CINCPOA). As CINCPOA, Nimitz held operational control of all USAAF assets in his theater, except for the XXI Bomber Command in the Marianas. (Public Domain)

Numbered air forces were typically subordinated to a theater commander, and so the Seventh Air Force's responsibility to CINCPOA was not unexpected. However, the Seventh Air Force also operated under intermediate commands throughout the 1943–45 Central Pacific campaign. Until June 1945 these too were always naval commands that encompassed all shore-based aircraft in the Central Pacific, regardless of branch. Indeed, as a major postwar study observed, "The Seventh Air Force was, in effect, a land-based arm of the Navy."

USAAF Major-General Willis H. Hale had first been assigned command of the VII Bomber Command headquartered at Fort Shafter, Hawaii on January 23, 1942. However, after the 7th Air Force's commander Major-General Clarence Tinker went missing on a raid on Wake Island, Hale was promoted to command the full 7th Air Force on June 20, 1942. Hale additionally served as an air officer in Lieutenant-General Delos C. Emmons' Hawaiian Department (US Army). Because the Seventh Air Force fought much of the war on a shoestring of manpower and resources, it was known as "Hale's Handful."

On August 12, 1943, Vice Admiral John H. Hoover was named "Commander, Land-based Air, Central Pacific." This title was changed to "Commander, Aircraft, Central Pacific" on December 1, 1943, before finally being modified to "Commander, Central Pacific Forward Area" on February 14, 1944. Hoover would remain in this position through the end of the war. Hoover had a complex reputation among his USN peers. On the one hand, he was universally regarded as being a highly competent and particularly aggressive officer. However, his personality was so prickly and off-putting that few US admirals wanted to work with him, while officers on his staff sardonically referred to Hoover as "Genial John" behind his back.

Hale was therefore subordinated to Hoover, and the two had a poor working relationship. This was partly due to Hoover's famously acidic personality. Mostly though the two commanders fundamentally disagreed on bombing tactics. As a USAAF-trained aviator, Hale believed in high-altitude level bombing runs. Hoover, however, was a USN-trained pilot who swore by dive-bombing.

The Seventh Air Force would face difficulties adjusting to the procedures of a unified command. In November 1943, Seventh Air Force tactical units would be assigned to Hoover's Task Force 57. As operations continued across the Central Pacific, Seventh Air Force units would be assigned to various USN task force commanders.

A native of Pittsburg, Kansas, Major-General Willis Hale commanded the Seventh Air Force in one fashion or another throughout most of the 1943–45 Central Pacific campaign. After beginning his career with the Philippine Constabulary, Hale was commissioned as a US Army officer in 1917 before earning his wings in 1923. (USAF)

Airfields

The Pacific War was largely a war to obtain land-based airfields. Most of these would be modified from primitive strips, if not carved out of virtual wilderness. Producing modern world-class airbases

Navy Seabees widen the runway at Eniwetok, April 1944. USAAF doctrine stated that heavy bomber operations generally required a runway at least 5,000ft long by 300ft wide. Eniwetok had been garrisoned by the 10th Marine Defense Battalion since late February, and by April about 11,000 Americans were on the atoll. (80-G-251475)

in as exotic and austere geography as the Pacific, often under fire, was a huge and thankless task, and it was filled by the highly skilled and dedicated aviation engineers of the USAAF and US Navy.

Most airbase construction in the Central Pacific was accomplished by Navy Seabees – military engineers recruited from civilians skilled in the construction trade. A single "Seabee" (Naval Construction) Battalion of 1,115 men (33 officers, 1,082 enlisted) could construct a small, advanced island airbase of the "Acorn" type. However, Seabees were often supplemented by USAAF aviation engineers, who were typically younger than Seabees (whose average age was 37) and were arguably better suited to prolonged labor and the occasional intense combat. Army engineers and labor units also provided much valuable effort in the general construction and maintenance of island bases.

Among the Pacific War's surprises was the great usefulness of coral as a construction material. Layers of crushed coral could be wetted and rolled into superb runways and taxiways of near concrete-level firmness; however, it had to be sprayed down daily to avoid heavy erosion. In addition to its direct use for airfields, crushed coral could also be used to build the causeways, piers, and roads required to facilitate an airbase's necessary logistics.

The deceptively simple pierced steel-plank Marston matting was one of the greatest technological developments of the war. Using Marston matting, a force of 100 unskilled laborers could lay down a 3,000ft long runway in 100 hours on almost any cleared terrain. Marston matting came in ten-foot-long strips of 15in. wide steel with interlocking edges. The strips themselves were a quarter inch thick, weighed 70lbs, and were pierced with large holes that reduced weight, provided friction for operations, and allowed water to drain quickly. The matting was normally laid down on 1–2in. of crushed rock or coral, but in emergencies it could be laid directly onto even soft, unstable ground. Marston matting was heavily mass-produced during the war and proved an extraordinary resource for American aviation engineers.

OPPOSITE AIR BASES IN THE GILBERT AND MARSHALL ISLANDS: NOVEMBER, 1943

As an example, on September 1, 1943 the USAAF's Hawaii-based 804th Engineer Aviation Battalion sent a detachment to primitive Baker Island. Over the course of ten days the battalion utterly transformed the tiny, previously useless rock into a major forward operating base boasting a 3,700ft long Marston matting-surfaced airstrip.

Seventh Air Force airbases often employed both USAAF and USN bulk fuel systems, which were interconnected. The USAAF bulk fuel system comprised the canvas Mareng cell and portable pipeline dispensing system, while the USN bulk fuel system was composed of ten 1,000-barrel prefabricated steel tanks revetted above ground, portable pipeline, four 5,000-gallon ready tanks, and dispensing system. The entire system was filled through a submarine pipeline tied into a tanker anchorage 2,000yds offshore.

Meteorology

The nature of regular long-range flight operations over the vast Pacific made dedicated meteorology a necessity. Unfortunately, Central Pacific weather tended to move from west to east, giving Japanese forces a natural advantage. By late 1941 the USAAF had activated the 7th Weather Squadron in Hawaii, comprising three stations in the Hawaiian Islands and one station at Christmas Island. By early 1942 the 7th Weather Squadron had established a necklace of detachments leading along the Hawaii–Australia air route.

The late 1943 Central Pacific offensive saw a new development in USAAF weather services. Previously, meteorology stations had largely been geographically fixed. But the Gilberts invasion saw the 7th Squadron develop mobile, pre-packed USAAF weather stations that were sent ashore with the assault forces. These could provide almost immediate service from newly captured airfields. In 1944 the Army Air Force, Pacific Ocean Areas (AAFPOA) would consolidate all weather services in the Pacific Ocean Areas under the 7th Squadron, which would evolve into the AAF Weather Services, POA by February 1945. However, local air commanders quickly found that standard USAAF meteorological service often had to be augmented by their own weather reconnaissance missions.

Long-range heavy bombers

The nature of the Central Pacific theater – its geography and its mission types – meant that the long-range heavy bomber was the backbone of Seventh Air Force operations. Beginning in late 1942, the Consolidated B-24 Liberator was the only heavy bomber type assigned to the Seventh Air Force. It flew most of the bombing missions during the 1943–45 Central Pacific campaign and was the only Seventh Air Force type capable of striking Japanese bases until the conclusion of the Gilberts campaign. This made the B-24 the workhorse of not only the VII Bomber Command, but the entire Seventh Air Force.

The B-24D had a top speed of 303mph and a service ceiling of 28,000ft. Cruising speed was 200mph. Combat radius was 400nm with a full bomb load of 8,000lbs. A medium bomb load of 5,900lbs bought an 800nm combat radius. The maximum efficient range of the B-24 was about 1,000 miles, which could only be obtained by limiting bomb loads to just 2,700lbs of ordnance. The B-24 was equipped with ten .50cal. machine guns for defensive purposes.

Despite the B-24 being the Seventh Air Force's primary offensive weapon, there was never any great fleet of heavy bombers available as there were in other USAAF theaters. In fact the Seventh Air Force seldom had more than a dozen squadrons of B-24s at hand. The average

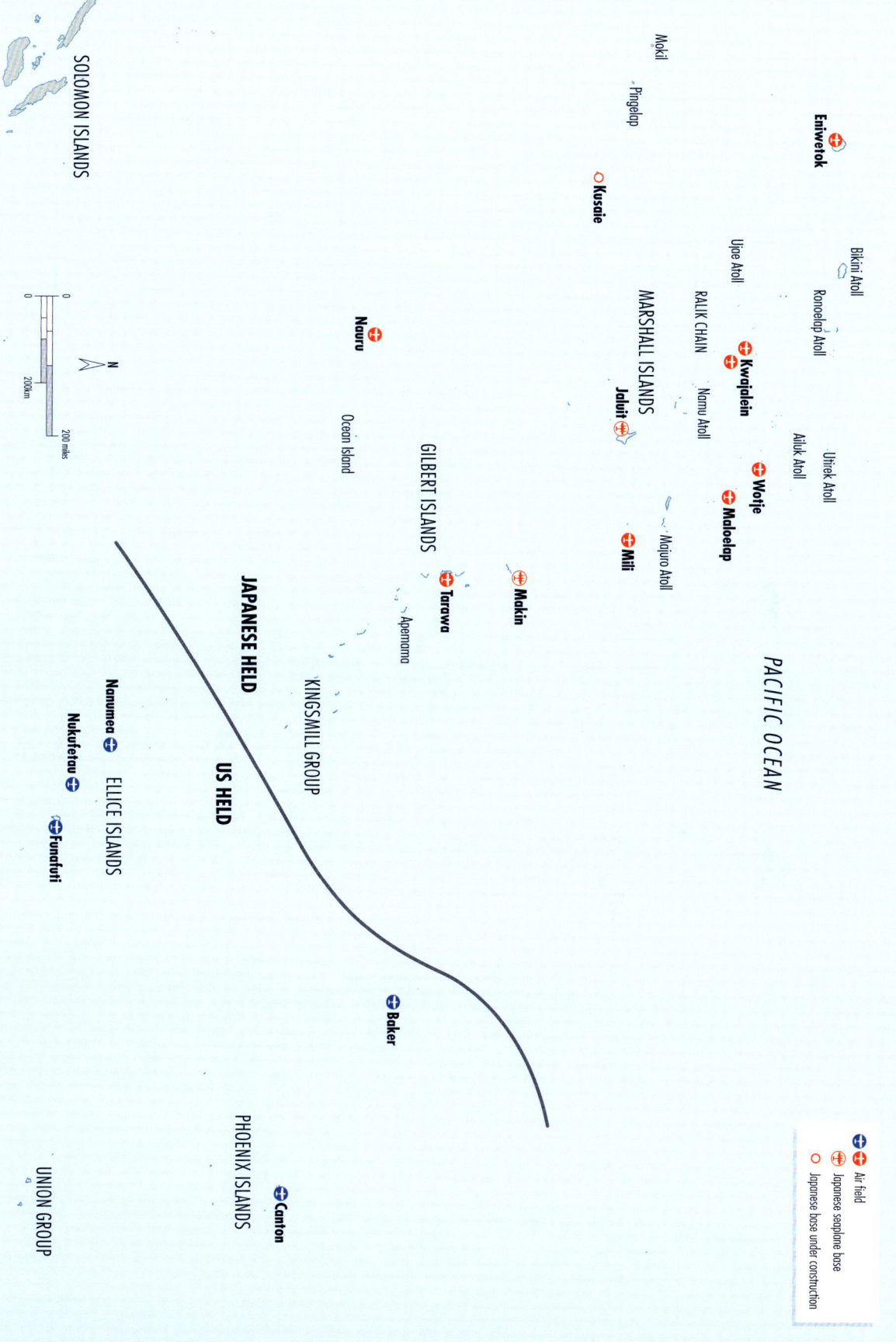

16 ATTACKER'S CAPABILITIES

Bolivar Jr, a B-24M of the Seventh Air Force's 11th Bomb Group (Heavy) viewed late in the Central Pacific campaign. Early-model B-24s were defensively weak in the nose. However, by 1943 the Hawaiian Air Depot had fitted over 200 Pacific B-24s with an ad hoc nose turret developed by the VII Bomber Command and would later provide further defensive firepower with the addition of belly- and tail-mounted twin .50 cal. machine gun batteries. Late model B-24s were fitted with these modifications in the factory. (Public Domain)

number B-24s available for combat in the forward area, between November 1943 and the end of the war, was 91.

Personnel	
USAAF Fighter Squadron	USAAF Heavy Bomber Squadron
(A-24, P-39, P-40, P-47, P-38, P-51)	(B-24)
25x fighters	12x Heavy Bombers
39x officers	67x officers
245x enlisted men	360x enlisted men
USAAF Fighter Group	USAAF Heavy Bomber Group
Group headquarters	Group headquarters
27x officers	25x officers
1x warrant officer	1x warrant officer
(3x Fighter Squadrons)	(3x Heavy Bomber Squadrons)
75x fighters	36x Heavy Bombers
117x officers	201x officers
855x enlisted men	1,080x enlisted men

Day fighters

In March 1941 the Hawaiian Air Force began receiving its first Curtiss P-40B Warhawk fighters. The P-40B's Allison V-1710 in-line engine powered it to a top speed of 352mph at 5,000ft. Unfortunately, the P-40 was crippled at high altitude by its single-stage, single-speed supercharger. Although lacking great performance, the P-40 was well-known for its toughness and durability.

The Seventh Air Force employed virtually every wartime variant of the P-40 at some point, finishing with Curtiss' final model, the P-40N. Produced in 1943–44, the P-40N featured a more powerful Allison engine, slightly longer fuselage, and better rearward visibility. Slightly stripped-down P-40Ns could reach 380mph. The P-40N model was armed with six .50cal. machine guns.

The Bell P-39 Airacobra began arriving at the Hawaiian Air Force in January 1942. The late-model P-39Q could maintain 375mph at 20,000ft, but performance fell off rapidly at higher altitudes. The P-39Q was armed with a 37mm cannon firing through the spinner, plus four .50cal. machine guns – two in the nose and two in the wings. However, the P-39 employed several unorthodox design elements for an American fighter, which did not endear itself to many pilots, nor did the P-39's reputation for deadly flat spins induced by the fighter's mid-mounted V-1710 Allison engine.

A P-47N Thunderbolt in the distinctive colors of the 413th Fighter Squadron, 414th Fighter Group, 1945. The 414th Fighter Group was the last fighter group to be assigned to the Seventh Air Force, deploying from Ie Shima in the final weeks of the Pacific War. (Public Domain)

By spring 1942 the Hawaiian Air Force had standardized entirely on the P-40 and the P-39. The P-40 and P-39 were slightly faster than the Zero at low altitude, while anecdotal evidence suggests the P-40 could outturn the Zero under certain low-and-slow conditions. At almost any other flight envelope the Zero far surpassed both the P-40 and P-39 in terms of performance, as both US fighters were limited by their single-stage, single speed supercharger, causing performance to drop off rapidly above 15,000ft. Both fighters would ultimately be replaced by newer high-altitude, high performance fighters. Nevertheless, the P-39Q would serve with the VII Fighter Command as late as early 1944, while the last P-40N Warhawk was only phased out of the Seventh Air Force in summer 1944.

In June 1944 the Seventh Air Force began receiving its first truly modern fighter, the Republic P-47D Thunderbolt. Driving the huge and powerful P-47D was the turbocharged Pratt & Whitney R-2800 Double Wasp air-cooled, radial engine. Top speed was 426mph at 30,000ft. The P-47D mounted eight .50cal. machine guns with 4,000 total rounds, while air-to-ground ordnance could include either two 1,000lb bombs, three 500lb bombs, or ten 5in. rockets.

The Seventh received its second modern fighter type in August 1944, when the 21st Fighter Group fully transitioned from the P-39 Airacobra to the Lockheed P-38L Lightning, with the 318th Fighter Group receiving P-38L Lightnings in November 1944. The Lockheed P-38L was a twin-engine, twin-boom, single-seat, long-range, high-altitude fighter. It was powered by two Allison V-1710 supercharged, counter-rotating in-line engines. Top speed was 414mph and combat range was 450 miles. The P-38 had four nose-mounted .50cal. machine guns and one 20mm cannon, allowing great accuracy and firepower. Up to 4,000lbs of bombs or rockets could be carried. Additionally, the P-38's two engines gave additional security for long overwater flights.

Very Long Range (VLR) fighters

The North American P-51D Mustang and later the Republic P-47N Thunderbolt were the first truly long-range fighters capable of escorting the B-29 raids to Japan and taking the fight to the Home Islands.

The legendary story of the P-51's wartime development needs little recounting here. Suffice to say, the belated combination of three disparate design elements in late 1943 produced a revolutionary aircraft previously considered impossible: a truly long-range, single-seat, single-engine fighter of superb performance that could not only escort US heavy bombers all the way from Britain to Berlin, but then dominate the skies over the German capital once it arrived. The three combining elements leading to the P-51's success over Germany were: 1) a superbly aerodynamic North American airframe (the P-51A); 2) the truly powerful two-speed, two-stage supercharged Rolls-Royce/Packard Merlin V-12 engine; and 3) the adoption of disposable drop tanks. The resulting hybrid was the revolutionary P-51B/C Mustang, introduced into the European theater of operations in December 1943.

OPPOSITE P-51D ESCORT TACTICS DURING B-29 RAIDS (SPRING 1945)

The diagram opposite represents a single P-51D group out of Iwo Jima on a VLR escort mission. There are three total squadrons of P-51D Mustangs escorting the B-29s. The P-51s loosely patrol up and down the B-29 bomber stream, and all are positioned well above the B-29 bomber string – whoever was above the target or defender had the tactical advantage, as all planes can dive faster towards danger than they can climb towards it.

The first P-51D squadron is 3,000ft to the port side of the B-29 bomber stream and 3,000ft above it. The second P-51D squadron is 3,000ft to the starboard side of the B-29 bomber stream and 3,000ft above it. The third P-51D squadron is slightly behind and slightly above the first two P-51 squadrons.

Although the P-51D was an excellent dogfighter, long-time US doctrine recognized the generally excellent maneuverability of Japanese single-engine fighters; their lighter wing-loading often allowed them to turn inside American fighters at many altitudes. In response, both the USAAF and USN had developed coordinated teamwork tactics to deal with the Japanese threat.

The first VII Fighter Command groups began transitioning to new P-51D Mustangs in December 1944. This improved Mustang introduced a bubble canopy, mounted six .50cal. machine guns instead of four, had a slightly redesigned wing and airframe, and was fitted with wing racks for mounting bombs. The P-51D had a top speed of 437mph at 25,000ft. When configured for Pacific VLR operations, the P-51D boasted a combat radius of 950 miles.

The Republic P-47N Thunderbolt was the last P-47 version to be produced in large numbers and was specifically designed with the greater ranges of the Pacific theater in mind. A major modification was its slightly larger "wet wings" stowing an additional 186 gallons of fuel – the wings themselves were visibly different with squared-off wingtips instead of earlier P-47's teardrop-shaped wingtips. A fully-fueled P-47N with drop tanks could carry a staggering 1,266 gallons of fuel, allowing an impressive ferry range of 2,350nm. The P-47N had a maximum speed of 448mph at 25,000ft and 460mph at 30,000ft. Combat radius in clean configuration was 800 miles.

Light and medium bombers

The shock of the 1940 blitzkrieg had forced the USAAF to hurriedly adopt a dive-bomber comparable to the Luftwaffe's Ju 87 Stuka. This was the Douglas A-24 Banshee, a USAAF version of the SBD Dauntless dive-bomber. The A-24B mounted two forward-firing .50-caliber machine guns and one flexible .30-caliber machine gun manned by the tail-gunner/radioman. Banshees were typically loaded with a single 500lb or 1,000lb bomb on its centerline and a 100lb bomb beneath each wing. The VII Fighter Command's 531st Fighter-Bomber Squadron, deployed to recently captured Makin Island, flew A-24Bs between December 1943 and March 1944, when it transitioned to P-39 Airacobras.

By November 1943 the North American B-25 Mitchell was the only dedicated USAAF medium bomber in the Seventh Air Force. The B-25 was especially heavily armed for strafing, mounting a 75mm cannon in its nose and a battery of .50-caliber machine guns. B-25s were used in low-level bombing, cannonading, and strafing missions against Japanese shipping and shore installations. The low-level attacks avoided radar, provided more accurate bombing, and facilitated strafing runs; but they could also be costly. The late model B-25J had a combat radius of 785 miles with a 4,000lb bombload. The Seventh Air Force operated the B-25 in the 41st (Medium) Bomb Group in four squadrons: the 47th, 48th, 396th, and 820th Bombardment Squadrons. The B-25s first deployed to the front in December 1943, flying from Tarawa and Makin.

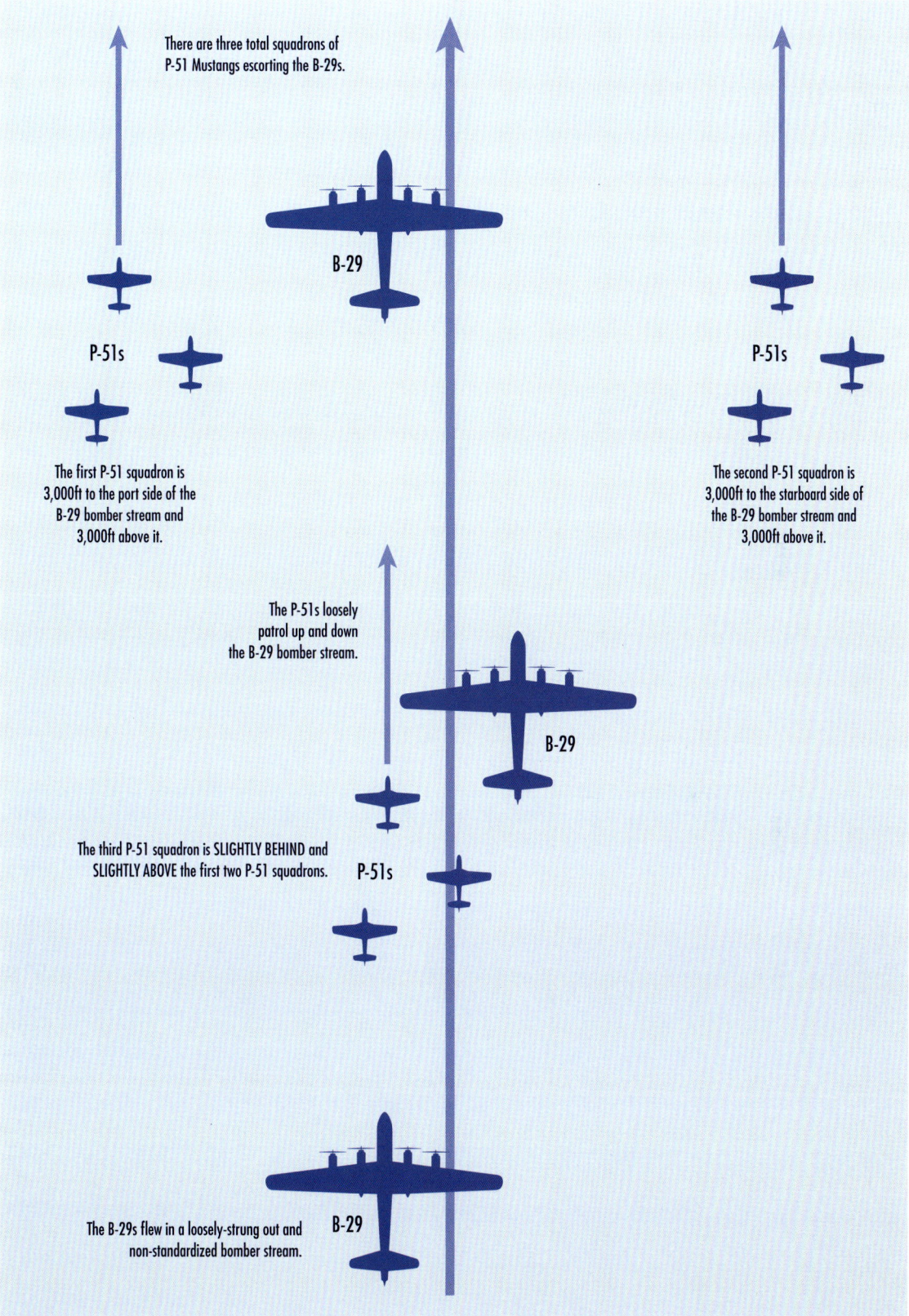

A B-25G Mitchell flying over the Army Air Force's Tactical Center in Orlando, Florida, April 17, 1944. The five-man Mitchell quickly evolved into a dedicated strafer; the B-25G seen here was armed with six .50-cal. machine guns and a nose-mounted 75mm M4 cannon. (USAF)

The 319th (Light) Bombardment Group, redeployed from Europe and re-equipped with the Douglas A-26 Invader, reached Okinawa in July 1945. The A-26 was fast (356mph), carried a large bomb load (6,000lbs), and mounted up to ten .50-caliber machine guns. So advanced was the Invader that it remained in USAF service until 1969, seeing action in the Vietnam War.

Defending Seventh Air Force airbases

An oft-overlooked role in the American island-hopping advance was the necessity to defend the newly won islands and airbases against potential Japanese counter-invasions and – more likely – harassing air or sea raids. The first US Central Pacific campaign conquests were defended by USMC defense battalions. By 1944 a USMC defense battalion comprised 1,386 men and was well-balanced between coastal and aerial defense. They were equipped with eight 155mm M1A1 coastal artillery guns, three batteries of 90mm M1A1 anti-aircraft guns, a searchlight battery of 12 searchlights, a battery of six 40mm M1 anti-aircraft guns, a battery of six 20mm Mk 2/4 anti-aircraft guns, and occasionally a tank platoon of 5–8x M3/M5 Stuart light tanks. Defense battalions were also equipped with early-warning and fire-control radar systems, M2 sound locators, M7A1B1 AA directors, and M1A1 height-finders. A slightly modified USMC defense battalion, the Airdrome Battalion, deleted the 155mm coastal batteries but increased anti-aircraft weapons to 12x 90mm M1 anti-aircraft guns, 12x 40mm M1 anti-aircraft guns, 12x .50-cal. anti-aircraft heavy machine guns, and 12x .30-cal anti-aircraft heavy machine guns.

US Army anti-aircraft artillery battalions also saw island defense duties. Gun battalions were armed with 16x 90mm M1s, while Automatic Weapons battalions deployed 32x 40mm M1 Bofors and 32x M51 or M55 quad-mount .50 caliber machine guns. A third AAA battalion type, the searchlight battalion, was equipped with 60in. searchlights, which could throw an 800-million-candlepower beam up to eight miles long and visible 50 miles away.

An SCR-527 radar set seen at Iwo Jima, 1945. The SCR-527 was a long-wave medium-range aircraft detector used for GCI (Ground Control of Interceptions). Designed to be mobile, the SCR-527 could be disassembled and transported overland by seven trucks. (Public Domain)

Defense from Japanese air raids required air search radar. The obsolescent SCR-270 ground-based air search radar served as the US Army's primary air search radar set through much of the war and would be seen at conquests such as the Marianas and Okinawa. It was supplemented by the SCR-268, which could be used for gun-laying or directing searchlights and had a range of 15–20nm. A more advanced air search radar was the AN/CPS-1. A single AN/CPS-1 radar set was shipped to Saipan in September 1944 but not immediately employed. Only after the late 1944 Japanese air raids was the AN/CPS-1 made fully operational and deployed atop Saipan's Mount Topachau, where it could detect enemy raids out to 120nm. Another radar set was the SCR-527, a mobile unit capable of directing interceptions against enemy aircraft.

Night fighters

The nighttime aerial interception of enemy aircraft was barely addressed by US aviation branches before the war. Night interception tactics were developed virtually from scratch via trial and error. Ideally, nighttime interceptions were guided from a ground-based control tracking the bogeys on radar.

Initially, P-39s, P-40s, and P-47s were all pressed into part-time, ad hoc night interception service. However, none possessed airborne radar. It was only the wartime development of practical airborne radar that made dedicated night fighters feasible.

Night fighters needed to be large enough to mount the necessary airborne radar, extra fuel, and additional navigational and communications equipment required for night operations. This meant night fighters were twin-engine and required several specially-trained crewmen to operate. Loiter time was important for maintaining airborne patrols, while a fast dash speed was required to make interceptions in time.

Much has been made of the relatively low air-to-air scores inflicted by US night fighters in the Pacific War, but this misses the point. Nighttime heckling by even a single Japanese bomber created unnecessary confusion, fatigue, sleeplessness, and lowered morale among men whose performance the following day would necessarily be negatively affected. And even

A Douglas P-70 Nighthawk in flight. The P-70 was an A-20 Havoc medium bomber that had been converted into a night interceptor. The Nighthawk was equipped with an SCR-540 radar set; its "arrowhead" twin-dipole radar antenna was mounted on the aircraft's nose. (Public Domain)

small Japanese night raids sometimes scored outsized damage to American assets, as would be seen in the Marianas in 1944 and Okinawa in 1945.

The Seventh Air Force night fighters' mission was therefore to patrol and deter nocturnal harassment raids by the Japanese, which came infrequently and rarely more than a few bombers at a time.

The Douglas P-70 Nighthawk was a night fighter version of the twin-engine A-20 Havoc medium attack aircraft. To modify the A-20s for night combat they were fitted with an SCR-540 airborne radar, four 20mm cannon in the nose with 716 total rounds, an additional 250-gallon internal fuel tank, and matte black paint on the forward airframe. The P-70 was always an interim solution until the arrival of a purpose-designed USAAF night fighter.

In May 1944 the 6th Night Fighter Squadron began receiving the USAAF's first dedicated night fighter, the highly advanced Northrop P-61 Black Widow. The P-61 was a twin-boomed, high-performance interceptor powered by two Pratt & Whitney R-2800-25S Double Wasp engines, each equipped with a two-speed, two-stage mechanical supercharger. Together they powered the three-man P-61 to a top speed of 366mph at 20,000ft, with a service ceiling of 33,100ft. The P-61's nose-mounted SCR-720 airborne radar had a range of five miles when operating in airborne intercept mode. The P-61 wielded plenty of firepower, mounting four forward-firing Hispano 20mm cannon in its lower fuselage, and four .50cal. M2 machine guns in a dorsal turret.

Carrier airpower

The Central Pacific island-hopping drive was a fully joint offensive comprising the US Navy, Army, Marine Corps, and Army Air Forces. All services provided a pool of assets to the campaigns' respective operational commander, regardless of branch. Although the Seventh Air Force never held operational control over US carriers, it worked in conjunction with them in a symbiotic relationship under the overall Central Pacific commander. A cursory understanding of US carrier power in the Central Pacific is therefore necessary to any Seventh Air Force narrative.

The USN's primary airpower contribution to the Central Pacific offensive was the Fast Carrier Task Force, which peaked at 17 fast carriers between late 1944 and early 1945. The USN's fast carriers could maintain 30kts in battle. Most were large and robust heavy carriers displacing about 30,000 tons and flying a standard Carrier Air Group of about 90 single-engine combat aircraft. These were overwhelmingly new Essex-class carriers but were joined by the older but similar *Enterprise* and *Saratoga*. Finally, nine fast carriers were converted light cruisers of the Independence class, which carried a smaller Carrier Air Group of 33 planes.

In contrast, escort carriers were small, slow (18kts), and unarmored aircraft carriers usually converted from merchant ships. An escort carrier air group comprised 20–30 USN planes. Escort carriers had three primary missions: amphibious air support, anti-submarine warfare, and aircraft ferrying. Up to 80 single-engine fighters or 54 twin-engine P-38 Lightnings could be ferried if the aircraft were to be unloaded at a port. If USAAF aircraft were to be delivered via a one-way takeoff, an escort carrier's capacity was about 40 single-engine fighters. Because USAAF pilots were never trained in the esoteric art of landing aboard a pitching aircraft carrier deck at sea, all USAAF fighters had to be loaded aboard the escort carrier by crane from developed port facilities. Once aboard, the USAAF fighters could be deployed from the escort carrier in one of two ways (both methods were one-way only).

If combat was imminent, or the receiving base still in a primitive level of operation, the escort carrier could steam within range of the objective airfield and launch the USAAF fighters from their flight deck Navy-style. This usually meant launching by catapult, a novel experience for USAAF pilots. When a USAAF fighter unit was loaded aboard an escort carrier, typically one or two higher-ranking members would, before departure, demonstrate a catapult launch to the rest of the unit to assure the men that it could be done and offer instruction for the remainder of the group. The launched fighters would then be reloaded aboard the escort carrier by crane. For the vast remainder of the fighter unit, their one-way launch from the escort carrier to the operational zone would be their first and only launch ever from an aircraft carrier.

Escort carrier USS *Casablanca* (CVE-55) ferries a deckload of 414th Fighter Group P-47Ns across the Pacific, July 16, 1945. The fighters had been loaded at Alameda Naval Air Station and were en route to Guam, where they would then be flown to Ie Shima. (Navsource)

The second method of unloading USAAF fighters from a ferrying escort carrier was to simply reverse the initial loading process and also unload them by crane at the destination. This was the preferred method, as it was less dangerous and – with no free flight deck being necessary for launch – allowed more fighters to be crammed aboard the same escort carrier on one trip. However, this method had two possible downsides. If the escort carrier was fully loaded for a crane-to-shore delivery, there was no way for the escort carrier or the embarked USAAF fighter unit to defend themselves – all defense would have to rely on escorting ships and aircraft. The second downside was that the use of a crane at the destination meant that the base the fighters were being ferried to required somewhat developed port facilities. These could be built surprisingly quickly in the forward zone by USN and USAAF engineers, even as combat still raged nearby. However, the urgency of combat operations meant that ground-based USAAF fighter strength was often required in the battle zone in the first few days of an amphibious invasion's initial landings, meaning a one-way flight to the recently captured or refurbished primitive air strips. Upon being launched from the ferrying escort carrier, the USAAF fighters would often have to fight their way into their new base, as return to the escort carrier was not an option. Upon landing, USAAF fighter pilots could expect only the most primitive of base services, either sleeping in tents or out in the open, and were often required to immediately dig fox holes and join in the armed defense of the airfield as auxiliary infantry until the ground situation became more stabilized.

Search and Rescue (SAR)

The sheer size and unforgiving nature of the Pacific Ocean made air-sea search-and-rescue (SAR) of downed airmen a top priority for the Americans. An extensive and capable air-sea rescue system naturally boosted morale, reduced fatalism, and encouraged more aggressive risk-taking in combat. Overwater SAR was pioneered by the US Navy, which always boasted a large contingent of seaplanes and flying boats in any forward area or overwater transit area. Several large flying boat types were also ubiquitous in the forward zones, where they were forward deployed at harbors or bays and often accompanied by seaplane tenders. Additionally, the USN also provided "lifeguard" submarines specifically assigned to the SAR role. These were deployed along planned ingress and egress routes and their positions made known ahead of time to air crews.

Long-range USN patrol bombers or flying boats performing air-sea rescue were designated "Dumbo" after the title character from the 1941 movie. In this case "Dumbo" referred to both the operation and the aircraft flying it.

Ideal Dumbo aircraft had extremely long-range, great loiter time, and robust radio capabilities, meaning they were often adapted from patrol bombers. Typically, heavy bombers would drop life rafts or lifeboats to stranded crewmen, while flying boats were often capable of rescuing crewmen outright. Dumbo aircraft could be dedicated specifically to the SAR role, or they could be patrol bombers pressed into Dumbo service for a specific mission.

The USN's best-known SAR aircraft was the highly versatile Consolidated PBY Catalina flying boat. The Catalina had a crew of eight and a cruising speed of 124mph. Its ubiquity, great loiter time, and ability to land on water made it the war's iconic SAR plane. However, the USAAF also developed its own overwater SAR capabilities. The USAAF version of the Catalina was called the OA-10A. By 1945 the Boeing B-17H, a specially-modified B-17 bomber, could drop to adrift airmen the Higgins A-1, a powered 12-man lifeboat. The USAAF additionally developed the B-29 Superdumbo specifically for the SAR mission, taking advantage of the B-29's extraordinary 14-hour endurance. A Superdumbo could drop pneumatic rafts, provisions, survival kits, and radios to airmen stranded at sea. Typically, two Superdumbos orbited on station north of lifeguard submarines, with another four on call at Iwo Jima. On August 14, 1945, a total of 14 lifeguard submarines, 21 USN PBY and PB4Y

seaplanes, nine B-29 Superdumbos, and five surface ships were on station in the SAR mission. In addition, surface craft were stationed off the ends of runways, USN patrol planes cruised offshore, and additional aircraft were on standby at Saipan and Iwo Jima in case of emergency.

A USAAF Consolidated OA-10A Catalina flying boat touches down in the ocean off Keesler Field, Mississippi, 1944. Its crew is undergoing joint training with the USMC. The versatile Catalina performed innumerable roles during the war and remains one of the conflict's underrated aircraft types. (Public Domain)

Limiting factors

The Seventh Air Force had to deal with unique factors that constrained its operations. Most were related to the Central Pacific's uniquely vast and empty geography. The myriad limiting factors typically compounded each other. Among the problems caused directly by Pacific geographical conditions were the great distances between islands in the Central Pacific, combined with the limited range of the Seventh's aircraft.

The Seventh would be required to deploy into advanced bases before adequate facilities could be established. The limited dimensions of most Central Pacific islands meant facilities were cramped and capacity limited. Additionally, an overall shortfall in shipping hampered the transportation of supplies to advanced bases. These factors combined to ensure a lack of sufficient maintenance facilities near the front.

The bases themselves were often out of range of the most desirable targets. Missions against targets that could theoretically be reached were handicapped by the problems of navigation over great distances, which were compounded by the dearth of navigational aids or landmarks. Inadequate weather forecasting often frustrated strikes or killed aircrew outright.

The Seventh also suffered from a general lack of airplanes, parts, and equipment, particularly radar-equipped bombers. However, there were often not enough aircrews either. During December 1943 the Seventh would lose 20 aircrews, but would only receive one combat replacement crew. For many months no replacement crews would be received. It was not until August 1944 that there were enough crews to man all available B-24 and B-25 bombers. The crews the Seventh received typically lacked adequate training, forcing the Seventh to establish schools teaching proper gunnery and navigation.

DEFENDER'S CAPABILITIES
Keeping the islands safe

A Kawanishi H8K Emily flying boat patrol bomber viewed from an American plane in July 1944 moments before the Emily was shot down. Both American and Japanese crews flew extremely long, mind-numbing patrol missions over the Central Pacific from their respective island bases. The boredom was tempered with the horror of going down a thousand miles from home. (Public Domain)

Commands

The entire Central Pacific theater fell under the operational purview of the IJN, in particular the IJN's main combat organization, the Combined Fleet. IJA units frequently bolstered the IJN's inherent island defense forces, but they were always under the operational control of the IJN until the final 1945 battles of Iwo Jima, the Ryukyus, and the direct defense of the Home Islands.

The US Central Pacific offensive had long planned to drive through the pre-war Japanese Mandates, which comprised the Marshall, Caroline, Mariana, and Palau Island groups. Together, these many separate archipelagos comprised a theater of truly awesome proportions, extending 3,000 miles west to east and 1,000 miles north to south. In December 1941, Japanese forces additionally conquered the northern Gilbert Islands to the east, the US-occupied Guam Island in the Marianas, and the US-occupied Wake Island to the Mandates' north. The IJN intended to use its Central Pacific island garrisons in an attrition strategy against the expected US counteroffensive. IJN island garrisons were primarily intended to stage air strikes. These islands typically had lagoons of sufficient size and depth to allow resupply by merchant shipping. In some instances harbors were large enough to shelter significant fleets.

The IJN was divided into numbered fleets for administration. As of November 1943, Vice Admiral Masami Kobayashi's IJN Fourth Fleet was a geographical command responsible for the Caroline, Marshall, and Gilbert Islands. Fourth Fleet's headquarters was at the bastion of Truk in the Carolines. Subordinated within Fourth Fleet was the IJN 4th Minor Base Force, headquartered at Truk, and the 6th Base Force, headquartered at Kwajalein in the Marshalls. The 4th Minor Base Force controlled the 41st and 42nd IJN Naval Guards units in the Carolines, while the 6th Base Force controlled six separate IJN Naval Guard units (numbered 61st through 66th), which garrisoned the Marshalls, Northern Gilberts, and Wake. All land-based IJN airpower was administratively assigned to the IJN 11th Air Fleet, which deployed its 24th Air Flotilla (*Dai-Nijuyon Koku-Sentai*) to the South Seas Mandates, where it fell under the operational control of IJN Fourth Fleet.

Japanese island defenses

An IJN Base Force or Special Base Force had no fixed organization but was assigned to the defense of a specific area, such as an island or an island group (*Tokubetsu Konkyochitai*). A Base Force might comprise aircraft, patrol boats, one or more Special Naval Landing Forces (SNLF), one or more Guard forces (*Keibitai*), pioneer units, and IJN civil engineering and construction units. Additionally, the Base Force was often augmented with heavy weapons such as coastal artillery and heavy anti-aircraft guns.

Vice Admiral Masami Kobayashi seen circa 1941–44. Kobayashi was assigned to command the IJN Fourth Fleet on April 1, 1943 and thus was the IJN's overall theater commander during the 1943–44 US invasions of the Gilberts and Marshalls. Kobayashi was forced into retirement on May 31, 1944 as a result of Fourth Fleet's inability to greatly slow or impair the US offensive. (Public Domain)

An IJN Special Naval Landing Force (SNLF) was a battalion-sized light infantry group led by an IJN commander. Multiple SNLF could be merged into a Combined Special Naval Landing Force, which roughly corresponded to a regiment and was commanded by an IJN captain or rear admiral. A mid-war SNLF on island garrison detail was ideally armed with 46 machine guns, eight 120mm coastal defense guns, sixteen 80mm anti-aircraft guns, four 75mm anti-aircraft guns, and numerous light anti-aircraft and anti-tank guns. A Guard force (*Keibitai*) was a unit of IJN naval infantry assigned to defend specific installations and was armed with light and medium anti-aircraft and heavy infantry weapons.

The IJN's quasi-military Pioneer units (*Setsueitai*), led by an IJN captain or commander, constructed airfields, barracks, fortifications, and similar installations at IJN-occupied islands. A Pioneer unit comprised 800–1,300 men, led by civilian and IJN officers of civil engineering background. Most manpower was Korean or Formosan civilian laborers. A Navy civil engineering and construction unit (*Kaigun Kenchiku Shisetsu Butai*) was the common labor unit. Ninety percent of its 1,000 men were Korean laborers, with the remaining ten percent armed Japanese overseers. As slave labor, these units' combat value was near zero.

IJN anti-aircraft artillery

Japanese early warning comprised three elements. Extensive numbers of visual observers could be used in rotating shifts at prescribed outposts, which were deployed as far forward as possible. Equipped only with binoculars, observers transmitted plane sightings by radio. Obsolescent trumpet-type sound locators were also employed, but these lacked effectiveness against modern high-performance aircraft. The third element was Japanese early warning radar, which remained primitive and lagged well behind American radar technology throughout the war.

The IJN had four models of dedicated anti-aircraft guns, ranging in caliber from 25mm to 80mm. The IJN also had several types of

A captured IJN Type 96 25mm anti-aircraft gun on Guam, 1944. The Type 96 was adopted in 1936 and while most went towards arming ships, several thousand were used as land-based weapons. As a medium anti-aircraft gun the Type 96 did not compare well to the American 20mm Oerlikons or 40mm Bofors. (National Archive)

dual-purpose guns. These were coastal artillery guns between 100mm and 127mm that could also be used as heavy anti-aircraft artillery. The most powerful of these guns had an operational ceiling of 25,000ft. Japanese fire control of both searchlights and anti-aircraft fire was primitive in 1943 but would greatly improve in 1944, with the occasional accurate anti-aircraft fire through overcast indicating the use of radar gun-laying. Additionally, a single Japanese fighter would often fly at the same altitude but well out of range of attacking US bombers and transmit fire direction data to Japanese anti-aircraft batteries.

Fighter defenses

Japanese aircraft were designed for extreme performance, but usually achieved this by forgoing self-sealing fuel tanks or cockpit armor, thus trading combat durability for extreme range and higher speed. Moreover, by 1943 Japan's ability to mass-produce state-of-the-art combat aircraft fell decisively behind the Americans and never caught up.

The Mitsubishi A6M Zero (Allied codename "Zeke") was the IJNAF's (Imperial Japanese Navy Air Force) standard fighter throughout the Pacific War. Although best remembered as a carrier fighter, the IJNAF also heavily deployed the Zero from shore-based IJNAF garrisons.

The Zero's agility far exceeded contemporary Allied fighters through late 1943. Its 1,100hp Nakajima radial engine powered it to a top speed of 331mph at 15,000ft, and gave it an excellent climb rate. The Zero was armed with two 20mm cannon and two 7.7mm machine guns. With its extreme long range the Zero also made a superb escort for IJNAF bomber strikes, and could carry a 550lb bomb in the fighter-bomber role.

The IJNAF's main fighter available to intercept B-24 night raids against the Mandates was the Nakajima J1N1-S Irving. The J1N1-S was a 1943 adaptation of the J1N1-C long-range escort fighter. The two-man night fighter variant employed four 20mm cannon, with

The Nakajima J1N1-S Gekko ("Moonlight") better known to the Allies as the "Irving," was an IJN night interceptor. Like the P-70 Nighthawk, the Irving was adapted from an existing twin-engine airframe. The J1N1-S defended Truk and would later intercept B-29s and P-51s over Japan. (Public Domain)

two firing upwards and two downwards. Maximum speed was 315mph at 19,000ft. The Irving was partly handicapped in the night interception role by the more primitive level of Japanese ground-based radar.

Counter-attacking air assets

By 1943 the backbone of the Mandates' organic counter-attacking force was the IJNAF's Mitsubishi G4M Betty bomber. The twin-engine Betty followed the usual Japanese practice of sacrificing armor to gain extreme performance. The Betty could carry 2,000lbs of bombs to strike a target 600nm away. The G4M's top speed was 266mph.

Also deployed in the Mandates was the Kawanishi H8K Emily flying boat, a large, four-engine maritime patrol bomber designed for extreme long range. It had a crew of ten. The Emily could carry 4,400lbs of bombs. The H8K2 model had a heavy defensive armament of five 20mm guns and five 7.7mm guns. Top speed was 290mph. The Emily was employed both as a long-range bomber and as a reconnaissance snooper. Its ability to operate from water gave it much needed versatility flying from primitive Mandates bases.

The IJAAF (Imperial Japanese Army Air Force) was little involved in the distant defense of the Central Pacific perimeter, but the Americans' June 1944 invasion of the Marianas finally put the US offensive in range of IJAAF counterattacks. The main IJAAF bomber in the late Central Pacific campaign was the Mitsubishi Ki-21 Sally, an obsolescent twin-engine bomber capable of delivering 2,200lbs of bombs. It had a crew of seven and a defensive armament of five trainable 7.7mm machine guns and one 12.7mm machine gun in a dorsal turret. Top speed was 301mph.

Defense of the Home Islands 1945

By 1945 Japanese radio intelligence monitored US signals from the Marianas, including weather reports. By careful analysis, Japanese intelligence could frequently divine the dates and sometimes even the targets of B-29 raids. However, Japanese defense of the Home Islands against aerial attack was predictably hampered by mediocre coordination between the IJAAF and the IJNAF. The two branches duplicated early warning efforts and did little to coordinate with each other. For example, in November 1944 the IJNAF had tentatively accepted responsibility for intercepting US aircraft approaching Honshu from the south and east, with responsibility confusingly shifting to the IJAAF once the American attackers made landfall, but the IJNAF maintaining interception responsibility for direct attacks against ports and its own IJN bases.

By 1945 the Japanese employed a total of 59 early-warning radar sets covering the main seawards approaches to Honshu, Shikoku, and Kyushu. Range was 150nm at best and resolution was poor. Japanese radar was unable to detect aircraft approaching at extremely high or low altitudes, or individual planes flying weather or reconnaissance missions. Altitude and formation were difficult to discern, meaning anti-aircraft artillery had precious little time to range on the attackers, while the presence of escort fighters could not be determined. Both the IJA and the IJN maintained separate networks comprising hundreds of visual lookout posts, although these were hampered by the mountainous geography of Japan. The IJN additionally deployed around 50 picket boats up to 300nm out to sea in these directions. However, visual sightings of incoming US aircraft were radioed on an IJN-only channel.

The IJAAF divided the Home Islands into multiple air defense districts. Fighters were expected to defend their air defense district only and were not required to reinforce a neighboring air defense district when it was under attack. This further exacerbated Japanese numerical weakness. Only 385 Japanese fighters were based in the Home Islands in February 1945, although this would increase to 450 fighters in April and eventually reach 535 fighters

30 DEFENDER'S CAPABILITIES

The Kawasaki Ki-61 Tony fighter was first used by the IJAAF in 1942 and was the only mass-produced Japanese fighter to use a liquid-cooled inverted V engine. This Ki-61 has been captured and is being test-flown at NAS Patuxtent River, Maryland in 1945. (Public Domain)

by August 1945. Nevertheless, rarely were more than 100 fighters operational throughout the Home Islands at any given time, with as little as 25 fighters operational in a specific air defense district. Additionally, lack of fuel meant Japanese fighter pilots were poorly trained; by July 1945 the average Japanese fighter pilot had only 100 hours of flight time to his credit.

Lack of interservice cooperation also plagued the anti-aircraft artillery. By 1945 the IJA had 1,250 anti-aircraft guns spread throughout the entire Home Islands. However, the IJN, defending only its own bases, deployed 980 heavy anti-aircraft guns and 3,700 25mm, 20mm, and 13.2mm automatic cannon. Repeated IJA attempts to borrow excess IJN anti-aircraft artillery to defend inland targets were rebuffed by the IJN.

Both services flew interceptor missions over the homeland in 1945. The increasingly obsolescent A6M Zero remained the IJNAF workhorse throughout the war, but by 1945 it had been overtaken in performance and durability by the N1K George fighter. The final Okinawa and Home Islands (*Empire*) campaigns in 1945 were the first time the Seventh Air Force faced large numbers of IJAAF fighters. Among these were the Nakajima Ki-44 Tojo, the Kawasaki Ki-61 Tony, and the Kawasaki Ki-45 Nick, a two-man, twin-engine heavy fighter.

CAMPAIGN OBJECTIVES
Dealing with distance

If the Pacific War was "a war of distances" then it is impossible to overstate the dominance of geography to the 1943–45 Central Pacific campaign. Simply put, the Pacific Ocean is vast. At its widest the Pacific Ocean stretches three-fifths of the way around the planet. Its waters occupy one-third of the planet and stretch across 13 time zones. Virtually all the cumulative landmass suspended within the Pacific lies on its periphery and is either classified as a continent (Australia) or lies within a few hundred miles of other substantial landmass (Japan, the Netherlands East Indies, the Philippines).

Central Pacific geography was daunting for airpower development not only because of its huge overwater distances, but also by the nature of its meager specks of land. The Ellice, Gilbert, Marshall, and Caroline island chains comprise low, flat atolls or small reef islands rising no more than 10 or 20ft above sea level. Most of these islands lack sufficient dry land to provide a single 5,000ft runway, let alone any space for dispersal, housing, or servicing areas. Many Seventh Air Force forward bases such as Nanomea, Makin, or Eniwetok were simply too small to base B-24s and could only support heavy bomber operations by functioning as staging bases. Additionally, World War II-era aircraft could only transport the most specialized cargo across oceanic distances. All bulky commodities required to build, supply, or defend Central Pacific airbases required transportation by ship – avgas (aviation fuel), food, construction equipment, heavy weapons, and so on. However, past Oahu, Central Pacific maritime port facilities were virtually non-existent.

A Seventh Air Force P-40E Warhawk of the 73rd Fighter Squadron, *Flagship Mary Ann*, prepares to launch from fleet carrier USS *Saratoga* (CV-3) on June 25, 1942. The 73rd Squadron was being transferred to Midway to replace the USMC fighters that had been nearly annihilated on June 4. (US Navy)

OPPOSITE BOMBING OF JAPAN: 1944–45

Air route	Distance
Los Angeles – Pearl Harbor	2,588 miles
Pearl Harbor – Tarawa	2,085 miles
Tarawa – Kwajalein	540 miles
Tarawa – Eniwetok	1,006 miles
Kwajalein – Pearl Harbor	2,415 miles
Kwajalein – Truk	1,097 miles
Kwajalein – Saipan	1,519 miles
Kwajalein – Eniwetok	369 miles
Eniwetok – Pearl Harbor	2,711 miles
Eniwetok – Truk	804 miles
Eniwetok – Saipan	1,146 miles
Saipan – Iwo Jima	723 miles
Iwo Jima – Tokyo	758 miles
Iwo Jima – Okinawa	853 miles
Okinawa – Tokyo	970 miles
Okinawa – Nagasaki	699 miles

After the Battle of Midway the Seventh Air Force was virtually stripped of strength to be sent to other theaters. From summer 1942 to just before *Galvanic* in November 1943 the Seventh Air Force never operated more than one heavy bomber group, and this was usually en route to or from another theater. However, on December 22/23, 1942 Hale was able to scrape together 26 B-24D heavy bombers from the 306th Group to stage through Midway and hit Wake Island. Surprise was complete but damage difficult to assess. Regardless, the use of staging bases to mount extreme long-range B-24 strikes over water would become a VII Bomber Command hallmark for the rest of the war.

Meanwhile Brigadier-General Robert W. Douglas Jr's VII Fighter Command was gearing up its own operations. In its mission as local island defense, the VII Fighter Command's strength had been increased from 200 fighters in August 1942 to 319 in October. Except for one squadron each of P-39s and P-70 night fighters, this force consisted entirely of P-40s. The VII Fighter Command operated out of several bases in the Hawaiian Islands, as well as one squadron each on Midway, Canton, and Christmas Islands. The 73rd Fighter Squadron had been specifically ordered to Midway in late June to replace the shattered USMC fighter Force that had taken the brunt of the Japanese attack. The 73rd's 25 P-40Es had reached Midway by flying off the carrier *Saratoga*. They would patrol Midway until January 1943, when they would be replaced by the 78th Fighter Squadron, which flew directly from Oahu to Midway.

Since January 1942 the Seventh had largely functioned in a training and replacement pool role. VII Bomber Command bombers would play the role of enemy bombers attacking Hawaii and would be accompanied by USN and USMC fighters playing the role of enemy escorts. The VII Fighter Command would then practice interceptions.

By October 1942 the VII Fighter Command comprised 300 fighters, all P-40s except for one squadron of P-39s and one squadron of P-70 night fighters. Most were deployed in the Hawaiian Islands of Hawaii, Kaui, and Oahu. Christmas and Canton Islands each received a fighter squadron. Since June 1942 the 25 P-40s of the 73rd Fighter Squadron had been deployed at Midway; they would be replaced in January 1943 by the 78th Fighter Squadron.

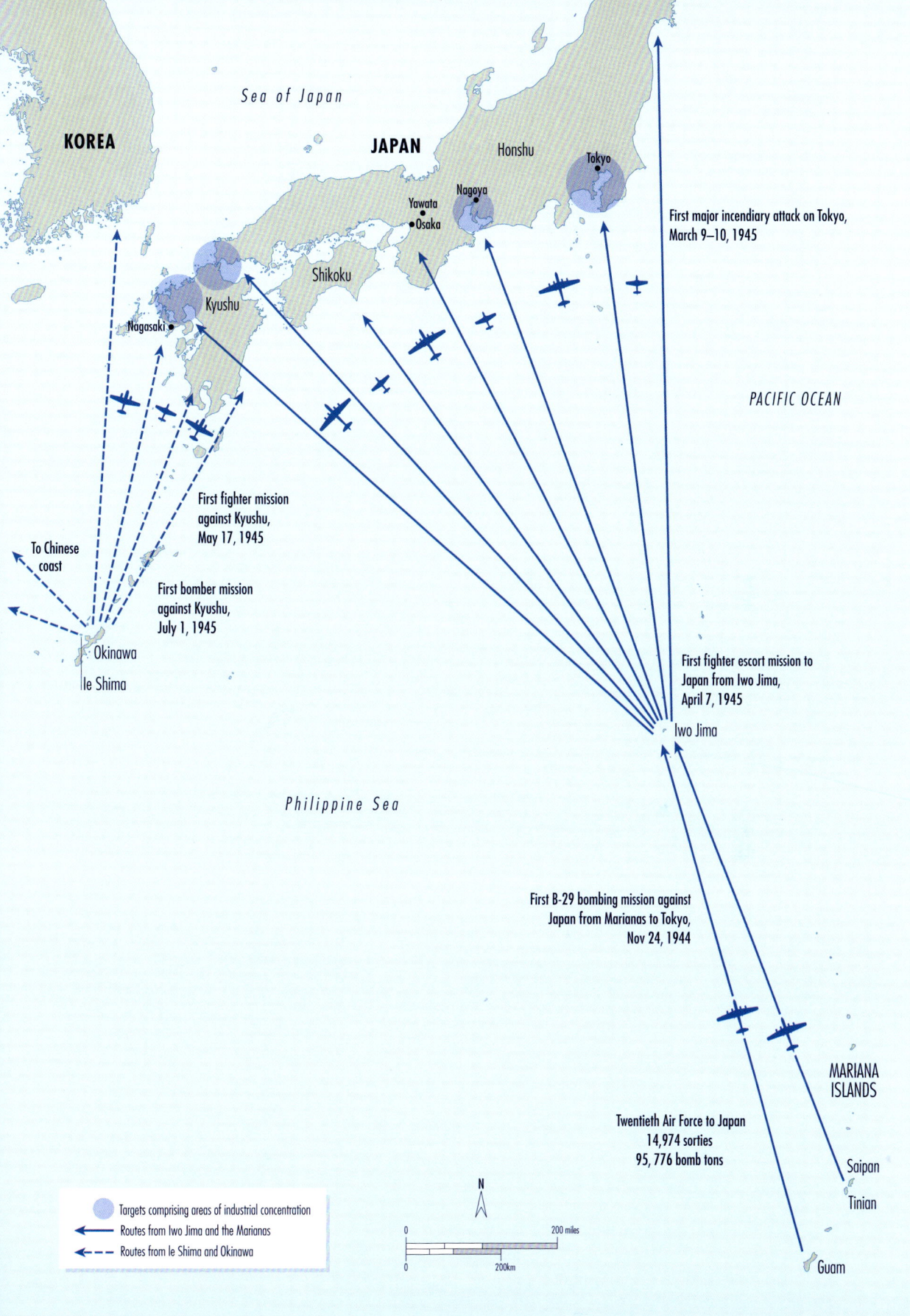

However, throughout 1942 and early 1943 the Seventh Air Force was constantly being siphoned from to provide reinforcements to the South-West Pacific Area. Between fall 1942 and fall 1943 the Seventh Air Force supplied an average of 25 trained fighter pilots a month to the Fifth and Thirteenth, while additionally transferring two fighter squadrons and a group headquarters to the Thirteenth. Such activity produced all the institutional issues inherent to severe personnel turnover.

Indeed Brigadier-General Walter Reed's VII Service Command was heavily tasked with much of the service and supply of USAAF units throughout the Pacific. Working with the Hawaiian Air Depot with which it was co-located in Oahu, VII Service Command functioned as a sort of all-purpose pit stop for any aircraft, personnel, and units transiting through Hawaii to forward Pacific theaters, regardless of parent command. Already by the end of 1942 the VII Air Service Command had over 40 Hawaiian warehouses stocked with thousands of aviation items, which it doled out as needed to anyone on its way to the South or South-West Pacific. The severe merchant and naval shipping shortage meant that the VII Service Command was providing a great complement of airlift to the trans-Pacific supply transport mission. However, because the Seventh Air Force owned no organic troop or cargo transport wing, this meant Pacific front supplies were simply stuffed aboard outbound bombers. In addition to the B-24 modifications listed earlier, VII Service Command also provided catapult launching and pressurization adaptations to the Seventh Air Force's P-39 and P-40 fighters, and later mounted rocket launchers on P-47s. The Hawaiian Air Depot naturally grew in size and importance throughout the war, and included increasingly large numbers of civilian workers, including women. However, by the preparations of the big Central Pacific offensive in summer 1943, the Hawaiian Depot would finally begin devoting an increasing proportion of its energies and resources to the Seventh Air Force itself.

Admiral Raymond Spruance, commander of the Central Pacific Force, in 1944. Spruance was a quiet, methodical man well-known for his excellent organization and deep intellect. Spruance was however leery of the Seventh Air Force after the USAAF's outrageously inaccurate claims at Midway. (Public Domain)

It was the Central Pacific Area that the USN had long intended to be the primary counteroffensive axis against Japan, and it accordingly received the lion's share of US naval assets. The primary formation conducting the Central Pacific counteroffensive was the Central Pacific Force, which Nimitz established on August 5, 1943 under the command of his trusted chief-of-staff Vice Admiral Raymond Spruance. The Central Pacific Force was a huge, self-contained formation consisting of three complementary forces: the Fast Carrier Task Force (high-speed battle fleet); the Joint Expeditionary Force (amphibious flotillas, amphibious air and fire support units, and embarked Marine and Army assault formations); and Defense Forces and Shore-Based Air (prefabricated forward bases, Marine defense battalions, and land-based USN, USMC, and USAAF air units). As the USAAF's Central Pacific formation, it was up to the Seventh Air Force to provide the USAAF's material contribution to the joint Central Pacific Force. However, this command arrangement would provide tension from the beginning. Although the Seventh Air Force had fought bravely and aggressively at the Battle of Midway, it had not actually inflicted any damage on the Japanese fleet, which was entirely destroyed by Spruance's and Fletcher's carrier air power. This would have been of little issue except that the Seventh Air Force public relations had beaten the USN to the media headlines, and falsely claimed the entirety of damage the USN had inflicted at Midway. Spruance was a cool and logical man, but he never forgave the Seventh Air Force for this, and would arguably be prejudiced against the Seventh throughout the Central Pacific offensive.

A P-47 of the 73rd Fighter Squadron takes off from USS *Manila Bay* (CVE-61) on June 23, 1944, shortly after the Aichi D3A Val dive-bomber attack. Four P-47s flew CAP over Manila Bay until the threat had passed, and then flew on to Saipan's Aslito Field to begin close air support operations. (NARA)

THE CAMPAIGN
Driving the Japanese back

Prelude: January–August 1943

The Seventh Air Force would refine its methods throughout 1943. On January 25, 1943, six B-24s of the 371st Bombardment Squadron staged through Midway and hit Wake again, this time in daylight. Despite six to eight enemy fighters scrambled, the B-24s escaped with mild damage.

With the CCS' increased interest in mounting a Central Pacific offensive, the Seventh Air Force was directed to launch two reconnaissance missions over the Gilberts in January and February 1943, followed by two Nimitz-approved strikes in April 1943. Nimitz combined the 370th and 371st Squadrons into Task Force 12, which would be staged from Funafuti nearly 2,000nm through Canton, Palmyra, and Christmas Islands.

Early on April 20, 1943, the Seventh Air Force launched a 22-plane B-24 strike from Funafuti against Nauru, damaging the island's phosphate works in a rare strategic attack by the Seventh Air Force. The following morning, the Japanese retaliated with their own air strike against the Funafuti airfield which severely damaged several parked B-24s. Regardless, Hale launched the planned second Gilberts raid on April 22, albeit a day late. Twelve B-24s struck Tarawa with seeming effectiveness. Hale refused to be caught on the ground a second time however and executed "the longest and fastest retreat in military history," having his B-24s safely back at Hawaii the following day. On May 15, seven of 18 B-24s sortied by the 370th and 371st Squadrons again hit Wake in daylight, inspiring a scramble of 18 Zero and four A6M5 Model 52 Hamp fighters. The Americans claimed four enemy fighters shot down but lost their first B-24 in action.

This period saw several reconnaissance runs over the Gilberts that brought back valuable intelligence. Then on June 27, some 19 inexperienced B-24s of the resurrected 11th Bomb Group flew down to Funafuti for a third Gilberts shuttle bombing mission. But two of the first eight B-24s to launch crashed, and subsequent launches were aborted. Of the six B-24s aloft, only two found the target. Although the intermittent raids did little permanent damage, they helped raise unit morale, broke up fatigue, exercised the combat and support elements

A Seventh Air Force B-24 bombs Nauru, circa 1943–44. Nauru is a small, isolated island 390 miles west of the Gilberts. Despite its size, Nauru was a major phosphate production center, with 810,000 tons produced in 1941 alone. Nauru was originally part of *Galvanic* invasion plans, but Nauru's rugged topography inspired the Americans to bypass it. (USAF)

of the VII Bomber Command, and provided valuable intelligence to US commanders. A final series of raids on July 24 and July 26, 1943 saw the 11th Bomb Group dispatch two separate, squadron-sized missions to Wake. The B-24s claimed a dubious 29 Japanese fighters shot down but lost one of their number in a mid-air collision with an enemy fighter.

However, in July 1943 plans for the Central Pacific offensive were revealed to Major-General Hale. Until now the Seventh Air Force had been flying from Hawaii in a strategic defense posture and mounting only occasional raids. Now Hale prepared to deploy his bombers hundreds and eventually thousands of miles forward with the objective of driving the Japanese back to their homeland.

From three airbases in the Ellice Islands, the VII Bomber Command had begun consistent attacks on Japanese airbases in the Gilberts. As events developed, this campaign to neutralize Japanese airpower continued all the way across the Pacific Ocean to Japan.

Gilbert Islands operation, November–December 1943

The long-term plan of the United States' Central Pacific offensive had been to occupy the Marshall Islands to use as a base to mount an assault on the IJN's major Caroline Islands bases such as Truk. However, reliable aerial reconnaissance of the presumably heavily-defended Marshall Islands could only be mounted from the adjacent Gilbert Islands. The Gilberts were already well-developed with airfields, so they could be used as a staging base for the Marshalls invasion, and they lay in a central location between the Central and South-West Pacific offensives. Accordingly, on July 20, 1943 the JCS ordered CINCPOA to invade the Gilbert Islands in late 1943, followed by an invasion of the Marshalls in early 1944. The Gilbert Islands landings, codenamed *Galvanic*, would be the first truly large deep sea amphibious operation in history. Because *Galvanic* set the basic framework for all future Central Pacific operations, it is worth studying in greater detail.

The strategic objective of Operation *Galvanic* was the occupation of the Gilbert Islands and the establishment of US air strength based on the islands of Tarawa, Makin, and Abemama. Tarawa was the focus of Japanese resistance in the Gilberts, however enemy airbases within the archipelago were within a few hundred miles of each other and formed a mutually defensive arc. Of these airbases, Maloelap was the best defended.

Galvanic's operational objectives were to capture the Gilberts atolls of Tarawa and Makin. To accomplish this, Nimitz had assembled the largest and most powerful US air-sea force yet seen, commanded by Vice Admiral Raymond Spruance and designated the Central Pacific Force. Making up Spruance's Central Pacific Force were several Task Forces, which were themselves comprised of subordinate Task Groups. Although the Central Pacific Force would be refined and tailored as needed to meet the demands of the moment (and enlarged as American industrial power increasingly allowed) the force's basic structure would remain through the end of the war.

US forces had never conducted a major amphibious assault directly into the teeth of fortified beach defenses. Combined arms doctrine for such an operation was therefore purely theoretical and still untested. A complicating issue was the assumption that the IJN Combined Fleet, based at Truk, would immediately sortie to counterattack as soon as it received word of the US landings. Therefore, the US plan, designed by admirals, emphasized surprise in order that the US fleet could quickly pivot to meet the expected IJN counterattack.

The Central Pacific Force's offensive spearhead was Vice Admiral Baldy Pownall's Fast Carrier Task Force (TF-50), comprising 11 fast carriers, 703 carrier aircraft, six fast battleships, six cruisers, and 21 destroyers. The amphibious assault fleet, Rear Admiral Richmond K. Turner's Joint Expeditionary Force (TF-54) was itself divided into two subordinate Task Forces. The Northern Attack Force (TF-52), also commanded by Turner, was assigned to assault Makin with 6,742 US Army troops of the 165th Regimental Combat Team (RCT) and a battalion of the 105th Infantry Regiment. The Southern Attack Force (TF-53), commanded by Rear Admiral Harry W. Hill, would assault the much stronger bastion of Tarawa with 18,600 marines of the 2nd Marine Division. The two Attack Forces boasted a combined eight escort carriers, 205 carrier aircraft, seven slow battleships, 11 cruisers, 21 destroyers, 22 transports, two LSDs, and three LSTs. When combined, the Central Pacific Force's elements afloat came to roughly 200 ships carrying 35,200 troops, 6,000 vehicles, and 117,000 tons of cargo to the battle area.

Rear Admiral Richmond Kelly Turner in early 1944. Turner was first assigned to command an amphibious force at Guadalcanal; Nimitz described him as "brilliant, caustic, arrogant, and tactless — just the man for the job." Turner was assigned command of Fifth Fleet's amphibious force in 1943 and retained the job throughout the war. (NHHC 80-G-216636)

In addition to naval and ground forces, the Central Pacific Force comprised a shore-based air element under Rear Admiral John H. Hoover (TF-57). Although *Galvanic*'s total air strength would mostly be provided by Pacific Fleet carriers, the Seventh Air Force would provide both bombers and fighters to the land-based TF-57. This Seventh Air Force element of TF-57 would be organized into two subordinate echelons. Seventh Air Force fighters were assigned to Brigadier-General L.G. Merritt's (USMC) Ellice Defense and Utility Group, designated Task Group 57.4 (TG-57.4). The Seventh's bombing force was designated TG-57.2 and put under the direct command of Major-General Hale. Two additional air groups, the 30th Bomb Group (Heavy) and the 41st Bomb Group (Medium) were transferred to Hale from the United States, reaching the theater in mid-October.

The Seventh Air Force's mission during Operation *Galvanic* was to deny the Japanese the use of their airbases in the Gilbert and Marshall Island groups on the islands of Tarawa (airfield), Makin (seaplane base), Nauru (two airfields), Mille (airfield), Jaluit (seaplane base), and Maloelap (airfield). Meanwhile, the Japanese airbases at Kwajalein, Roi, and Wotje were assigned to USN air.

The Seventh Air Force supported Operation *Galvanic* with seven heavy bomber squadrons (about 80 B-24s) and three fighter squadrons, all flying from the five islands of Canton, Funafuti, Nukufetau, Nanomea, and Baker. These islands were not only small and austere, but lay up to 2,000nm forward from the Seventh Air Force's Hawaiian Air Depot. Additionally, the range to the target was so great that except for two squadrons based at Nanomea, all B-24s would have to stage through Nanomea and Baker.

Of the five forward airbases assigned to the VII Bomber Command, only Canton and Funafuti were already developed. Canton had two airstrips of compacted guano and coral, one 7,200ft long and the second 9,400ft long. Funafuti had a 6,000ft runway of crushed coral.

At the remaining sites of Nukufetau, Nanomea, and Baker, Seabees and aviation engineers toiled to build airstrips created specifically for *Galvanic*. In September 1943, 19 P-40N fighters of the VII Fighter Command flew from Canton to Baker to provide defense for the engineers, who carved the necessary 6,000ft runways out of coconut groves.

To prevent Japanese interference with the airbases' construction, a joint USN/USAAF strike was planned against Tarawa Atoll, which had an operational 4,000ft airstrip on the island of Betio. The 11th Bomb Group supplied one heavy bomber squadron each to Major-General Landon's Canton Air Group (12 B-24s, six PBYs) and Brigadier-General Harold D. Campbell's (USMC) Funafuti Air Group (12 B-24s, 12 PBYs, 10 PV-1s). The night of September 18, 1943, 18 of the 24 Liberator bombers dispatched successfully

ORDERS OF BATTLE: OPERATION *GALVANIC*, NOVEMBER 1943

UNITED STATES
US CENTRAL PACIFIC OCEAN AREA – ADMIRAL CHESTER W. NIMITZ
USAAF SEVENTH AIR FORCE – MAJOR-GENERAL WILLIS HALE (FUNAFUTI)
VII Bomber Command
VII Fighter Command
VII Service Command
19th Troop Carrier Squadron – used for air transportation of personnel and emergency supplies

US CENTRAL PACIFIC FORCE – VICE ADMIRAL RAYMOND SPRUANCE (*INDIANAPOLIS*)
Task Force 50 – Carrier Force – Vice Admiral Baldy Pownall
Six fleet carriers, five light carriers, six fast battleships, three heavy cruisers, three anti-aircraft light cruisers, 21 destroyers
Task Force 54 – Joint Expeditionary Force – Rear Admiral Richmond K. Turner
Task Force 52 – Northern Attack Force (Makin)
Three escort carriers, four old battleships, four heavy cruisers, 15 destroyers, one minesweeper, five transports, four landing ships
Task Force 53 – Southern Attack Force (Tarawa)
Five escort carriers, three old battleships, two heavy cruisers, two light cruisers, 22 destroyers, two minesweepers, 16 transports, four landing ships
V Amphibious Corps – Maj. Gen. Holland M. Smith
Tarawa: 2nd Marine Division – Maj. Gen. Julian C. Smith
Makin: 27th Infantry Division (Army) – Maj. Gen. Ralph C. Smith
Task Force 57 – Shore-Based Air – Rear Admiral John H. Hoover (Aircraft tender *Curtiss*, anchored in Funafuti)
Task Group 57.2 – Striking Group – Major-General Willis Hale (Funafuti)

VII BOMBER COMMAND – MAJOR-GENERAL WILLIS HALE
11th Bomb Group (B-24s) (Funafuti)
26th Heavy Bombardment Squadron (Canton)
42nd Heavy Bombardment Squadron (Funafuti)
98th Heavy Bombardment Squadron (Nukufetau)
431st Heavy Bombardment Squadron (Funafuti)
30th Bomb Group (B-24s) (Nanomea)
27th Heavy Bombardment Squadron (Nanomea)
38th Heavy Bombardment Squadron (Nanomea)
392nd Heavy Bombardment Squadron (Canton)
45th Fighter Squadron (P-40s) (Baker)
46th Fighter Squadron (P-39s) (Canton)
531st Fighter Bomber Squadron (A-24s) (Canton)
1st ASSRON (Baker)
3rd ASSRON (Funafuti)
Detachment, 3rd ASSRON (Nanomea)
Detachment, 3rd ASSRON (Nukufetau)
Detachment, 17th AB Squadron (Canton)
422nd Sub-Depot (Canton)

TASK GROUP 57.4 ELLICE DEFENSE AND UTILITY GROUP – BRIGADIER-GENERAL L.G. MERRITT (USMC)
15th Fighter Group
6th Fighter Squadron
18th Fighter Squadron
47th Fighter Squadron
78th Fighter Squadron
318th Fighter Group
19th Fighter Squadron
72nd Fighter Squadron
73rd Fighter Squadron
333rd Fighter Squadron

JAPAN
COMBINED FLEET, TRUK
1st Battleship Division, Commandant (Headquarters, Combined Fleet)
Battleships *Yamato*, *Musashi*
2nd Fleet, Commander-in-Chief – Vice Admiral Nobutake Kondo
4th Squadron
Heavy cruisers *Atago*, *Takao*, *Maya*, *Chokai*.
5th Squadron
Heavy cruisers *Myoko*, *Haguro*.
2nd Destroyer Squadron
Noshiro, unknown number of destroyers
3rd Fleet, Commander-in-Chief – Vice Admiral Shiro Takasu
3rd Squadron
Battleships *Kongo*, *Haruna*
7th Squadron
Heavy cruisers *Kitmano*, *Suzuya*, *Tone*, *Chikuma*
10th Squadron
Light cruiser *Yahagi*, unknown number of destroyers
4th Fleet, Commander-in-Chief, Truk – Vice Admiral Masashi Kobayashi
14th Squadron
Light cruisers *Naka*, *Isuzu*, *Nagara*
4th Minor Base Force Commandant, Truk
41st Naval Guards, Truk
42nd Naval Guards, Ponape

6th Base Force Commandant, Kwajalein
61st Naval Guards, Kwajalein
62nd Naval Guards, Jaluit
63rd Naval Guards, Wotje
64th Naval Guards, Moloelap
65th Naval Guards, Wake
66th Naval Guards, Mille

6th Fleet, Commander-in-Chief, Truk – Admiral Takeo Takagi
1st Submarine Squadron
Approximately 18x submarines

Japanese aircraft numbers on Truk		
Unit	Type	Numbers/Locations
755th Kokutai	Mitsubishi G4M Betty	25x (Ruotto) 9x (Maloelap) 6x (Nauru)
252nd Kokutai	Mitsubishi A6M Zero	21x (Taroa) 9x (Kwajalein)
352nd Kokutai	Yokosuka D4Y Judy	18x (Mille)
801st Kokutai	Kawanishi H8K Emily	8x (Jaluit)
6th Base Force: 952nd Kokutai	Mitsubishi F1M2 Pete	3x (Makin) 9x (Kwajalein)
4th Base Force: 902nd Kokutai	Mitsubishi F1M2 Pete	9x (Truk) 3x (Saipan)
Total: 120		

Number of Japanese personnel on Truk
Tarawa – Rear Admiral Shibasaki (5,000 total personnel)
3rd Special Base Defense Force
Saesbo 7th Special Naval Landing Force (SNLF)
111th Construction Unit
Detachment, 4th Fleet Construction Department
Makin
Special Naval Landing Force (284 troops) – Lieutenant Junior-Grade Seizo Ishikawa
111th Pioneers (138 men) – Lieutenant Kurokawa
4th Construction Unit (76 Japanese and 200 Korean laborers)
(plus 100 aviation personnel)
Apamama
20 garrison troops

Strength of the most Important Japanese garrison islands in the Central Pacific, January 15, 1944	
Eniwetok Atoll	1,000 garrison troops
Jaluit Atoll	3,500 garrison troops
Kwajalein Atoll	8,000 garrison troops
Maloelap Atoll	3,300 garrison troops
Kusaie Island	4,000 garrison troops
Mille Atoll	5,500 garrison troops
Nauru Island	6,000 garrison troops
Ponape Island	5,000 garrison troops
Truk Atoll	20,000 garrison troops
Wake Island	6,700 garrison troops
Wotje Atoll	3,500 garrison troops
Unknown	6,000 garrison troops
TOTAL	72,500 garrison troops

hit Tarawa's airfield with frag clusters and GP bombs. The following morning, the fast carriers *Lexington*, *Belleau Woods*, and *Princeton* struck Tarawa with minimum aerial interference. They were followed by a return bombing/photoreconnaissance strike of 20 B-24s, which suddenly encountered heavy flak and 15–20 A6M Zeros. One B-24 was lost and ten damaged.

At Nukufetau, a Seabee detachment would surface a 6,100ft bomber strip and 3,500ft fighter strip by D-Day, complete with hardstands, revetments, and parking areas that could accommodate 45 fighters and 34 bombers. Nukufetau also received a control tower, radio station, and weather station. At Nanomea a 7,000ft bomber and 3,000ft fighter strip were ready by D-Day, as well as first echelon maintenance facilities such as a nose hangar and repair shops. Further amenities included a control tower and portable boundary lights on one side of the bomber runway. At Baker the Seventh Air Force's 804th Engineer Aviation Battalion had constructed a 5,500ft runway covered by steel Marston matting and included hardstands and a parking mat for 25 fighters and 24 heavy bombers.

Planning, preparation, training, security precautions, and logistic responsibilities of Seventh Air Force striking elements fell to its own USAAF staff, even as the USN exercised operational control. This lack of operational authority required the Seventh Air Force to be

Nanomea in the Ellice Island group was occupied by the 7th Marine Defense Battalion on August 18, 1943. Engineers had built adequate airfield facilities by late September and the island was staging air raids the following month. Several US Navy F4F Wildcat fighters are seen here at the Nanomea airfield in October 1943. (Public Domain)

prepared to execute any type of mission on short notice. Supporting the combat units in their forward areas required much ingenuity and improvisation.

Ground crews accompanied the flight personnel to the forward islands, allowing first- and second-level aircraft maintenance. More advanced maintenance in these forward areas was not immediately practical, especially as they were up to 2,000nm from the Hawaiian Air Depot. To rectify this, Seventh Air Force Service Command developed the Air Service Support Squadrons (ASSRONS) concept.

ASSRONS' duties were listed as "repair, supply, evacuation, sanitation, construction, transportation, traffic control, salvage, graves registration, burials, quartering, training of service units, estimation and supervision of funds, and other activities as may be required."

The ASSRON was a short-lived phenomenon born partly from the need to operate under chronic personnel shortages in late 1943. By February 1944 this would largely be overcome and the ASSRON concept would be abandoned in favor of standard service groups.

By October 1943, the Several Air Force's 45th Fighter Squadron had occupied Baker Island, relieving the ISN garrison there. On October 23, a bogey was detected on radar and two P-40Ns scrambled to intercept. They ultimately shot down a snooping Emily flying boat – the VII Fighter Command's first aerial victory since Pearl Harbor.

In November 1943, four total IJN air groups were deployed in the Gilberts and Marshalls. These comprised 34 G4M Betty bombers, 30 A6M Zero fighters, 18 D4Y Judy dive-bombers, eight H8K Emily flying boats, and five F1M2 Pete seaplanes. A sixth IJN air group comprising 12 F1M2 Petes was deployed at Truk and Saipan. Although additional Japanese planes could be staged from Japan and other strongholds through the Pacific Islands to reinforce the Mandates, by 1943 organic Japanese airpower in the Central Pacific was horribly outnumbered by US carrier airpower alone, never mind attached USAAF strength.

Indeed, total US air strength available to initiate *Galvanic* strikes comprised 908 single-engine carrier aircraft and 80 B-24 heavy bombers from the VII Bomber Command. Additional fighters and auxiliary aircraft remained in the Ellice Islands but were unable to participate offensively. Rear Admiral Hoover would command the entire TF-57 from the seaplane tender USS *Curtiss*, anchored in Funafuti's lagoon and connected via telephone, teletype, and FM radio to all outlying TF-57 bases.

Air strikes began on November 13, 1943 (D-7) when 18 B-24s from Funafuti's 11th Bomb Group raided Tarawa. They unloaded 126x 20lb frag clusters and 55x 500lb bombs,

Vice Admiral Hoover's flagship for Operation *Galvanic*, seaplane tender USS *Curtiss* (AV-4), seen upon commissioning in November 1940. Hoover's decision to make his headquarters afloat instead of ashore is perhaps telling of his feelings towards land-based airpower. (Public Domain)

losing one B-24 to unknown causes. The B-24s returned to Tarawa in force on November 14, November 17, and November 19. Carrier strikes hammered both Tarawa and Makin between November 16 and November 19 (D-1) with B-24s also hitting Makin on D-1.

However, the B-24s' primary mission was to hammer Japanese airbases, of which there were many. The B-24s hit both Mille and Tarawa on D-6, followed by Jaluit and Mille on D-5, and then worked over Kwajalein and Maloelap on D-4. Tarawa and Mille were again struck on D-3, while poor weather forced the D-2 attacks against Wotje to be diverted back to Mille and Tarawa. However, back on November 12 the IJN had transferred 27 G4M Betty bombers to Rabaul on November 12, meaning only 46 Japanese aircraft remained in the entire Gilberts–Marshalls area even as the B-24 attacks began.

The B-24s were flying perhaps the longest combat missions ever attempted until the arrival of the B-29, with a maximum round-trip range of over 2,400 miles. With virtually no landmarks available en route and both the bases and targets the tiniest of islands, navigation was at a premium. Unsurprisingly, operational dangers exceeded those of actual combat.

The amphibious assault was scheduled for November 20, 1943. By D-Day, Seventh Air Force B-24s had dropped 116.5 tons of GP bombs and 5,634 20lb fragmentation bombs on Japanese defenses throughout the Gilberts and Marshalls, with six missions unloading 50 tons of ordnance against the one-square-mile island of Betio, the strongpoint of resistance on the Tarawa Atoll. Five B-24s had been lost in the air and two on the ground to Japanese attacks, totaling 17 killed or missing and 19 wounded. Aerial combat had resulted in the downing of five to ten Japanese planes. The combined attacks of Seventh Air Force and USN carriers reduced Japanese aerial opposition to negligible levels, although the Japanese were able to mount four air attacks against Seventh Air Force bases.

Early on November 20, 1943, Hill's Southern Attack Force (TF-53) opened its troubled and ineffective D-Day naval bombardment of Tarawa of just two and a half hours, with over an hour and a half pause to allow a belated carrier airstrike. Over 80 percent of the pre-invasion bombardment of Tarawa had been by naval guns, with B-24s and carrier aircraft contributing just 10 percent each. Tarawa's low, flat coastline also foiled the flat trajectory of the point-blank range naval bombardment. The marines were forced to storm directly into withering defensive fire, even as their landing craft foundered hundreds of yards out on coral reefs. Major communications foul-ups proved costliest of all, as Hill's flagship, battleship *Maryland*, immediately disabled all her radio communications with her first 14in. salvo. Top US commanders therefore spent much of D-Day unable to communicate at all. Despite overwhelming advantages in matériel and firepower, the issue at Tarawa was

A Seventh Air Force B-24 Liberator flies over its target, the bypassed island of Wotje, circa 1943–44. Wotje was a large atoll in the Marshall Islands, with dry land for a large airfield and a huge, deep lagoon capable of anchoring 2,000 ships. Wotje also boasted a seaplane base and developed fortifications but was ultimately bypassed by US invasion forces and suppressed into irrelevance by the Seventh Air Force. (USAF)

in doubt for much of D-Day. Betio was only gruelingly conquered by November 23 at the cost of 1,009 Americans dead.

Off Makin, Turner's Northern Attack Force (TF-52) also encountered heavy resistance, requiring methodical direct attacks. However, Makin too was declared secure on November 23, costing 64 US troops killed.

The Japanese retaliated with airstrikes. Late on D-Day, sixteen G4M Betty bombers from Roi and Maloelap attacked Pownall's fast carriers. Eleven Bettys were shot down, but light carrier *Independence* took a torpedo, killing 17. She retired for repairs at Funafuti.

Beginning on November 23 the Japanese flew 68 planes up from Truk to Roi. Their first counterattack came late on November 25, when thirteen G4M Betty bombers attacked Turner's Northern Attack Force without success. A second group of Japanese planes raiding Pownall's carriers was also repulsed, as was a third strike the following night. Thanks to US neutralization raids, Japanese aerial counterattacks proved a failure. Far more successful was a Japanese submarine attack on November 24, which claimed 644 US sailors by sinking escort carrier USS *Liscome Bay* (CVE-56).

Between November 13 and December 6, 1943, the Seventh Air Force had struck the Gilbert Islands on 14 missions: Tarawa six times, Makin three times, and Nauru five times. The Seventh Air Force had also executed 15 missions against the Marshall Islands, including eight strikes against Mille, three against Jaluit, and four against Maloelap, for a total of 29 missions against the Marshalls and Gilberts. A total of 325 tons were dropped in 279 effective sorties, all by B-24 bombers. Between USN carrier strikes, the Seventh's B-24 raids, and attrition from their own attacks, the Japanese had lost a total of 122 planes in the Marshall Islands between November 13 and December 13.

Although the Americans had made many costly tactical errors during *Galvanic*, these failures would be carefully studied and corrected for subsequent operations. Indeed, once improved, *Galvanic* provided the basic model for US Central Pacific amphibious operations for the rest of the war. However, not only would doctrine improve, so would the Central Pacific Force accumulate progressively more operational experience while also growing to staggering proportions.

The Marshall Islands operation, January–March, 1944

The strategic objectives of the Marshall Islands operation were to be accomplished in two phases. The first phase was the capture of Kwajalein and Majuro Atolls (Operation *Flintlock*), while the second would be the capture of Eniwetok Atoll (Operation *Catchpole*). However, so far as the Seventh Air Force was concerned, operations between *Galvanic* and *Flintlock/Catchpole* were continuous.

The Marshalls drive would see Major-General Hale's Seventh Air Force remain a part of Rear Admiral Hoover's Task Force 57. For the assault on Kwajalein, the Seventh Air Force was to neutralize Japanese airbases at Mille and Jaluit. This would occur preceding, during, and subsequent to the invasion of Kwajalein and Majuro. Additionally, the Seventh Air Force would destroy any Japanese aircraft and facilities at Maloelap, Wotje, Roi, and Kwajalein. Beginning on D-2, Seventh Air Force would assist naval forces in denying Wotje and Maloelap to Japanese reinforcements. The Seventh Air Force would also target Japanese shipping present. Finally, on D-Day, February 1, 1944, B-24s would

US Navy Seabees hurriedly construct a new airfield at Tarawa's Betio Island shortly after its capture, November 1943. The runway would be operational just a few weeks later, with a second runway completed in January 1944. (NHHC 80-G-57388)

drop 2,000lb bombs against Japanese defenses on Kwajalein in direct air support of the amphibious assault.

For the assault against Eniwetok, the Seventh Air Force was assigned to neutralize Japanese airbases at Ponape and Kusaie. At the same time, they would continue to suppress Japanese airpower at Mille, Jaluit, Maloelap, and Wotje.

After the attrition of the Gilberts campaign, the IJN's 22nd Kokutai had 128 planes based in the Marshalls, of which 35 were deployed at Roi-Namur, ten at Kwajalein, nine on Wotje, 59 on Maloelap, and 15 at Eniwetok.

Forces available for the Seventh Air Force included six heavy bombardment squadrons, four medium bombardment squadrons, three fighter squadrons, and one dive-bomber squadron. The primary objectives would be aircraft and shipping, with continuous day and night operations focusing against important Japanese airbases and ground installations.

Meanwhile, the Makin Garrison Group of four merchantmen and two destroyer-escorts would arrive off Makin on November 24. At Makin, Seventh Air Force aviation engineers would quickly complete Starmann Field, which boasted a 7,000ft runway partially surfaced in steel Marston matting, dispersal areas for 78 fighters and 24 heavy bombers, and third-echelon maintenance facilities.

Similarly, the Tarawa Garrison Group of four merchantmen and two destroyer-escorts would arrive off Betio on November 25. The convoy carried 1,900 men, including a Seabee detachment to build a standard "Acorn" airbase. However, airfield development at Tarawa and Apamama went slower than planned. Tarawa received two B-25 squadrons from the 41st Bomb Group on December 15, although Tarawa airfields were not truly operational until December 23. When Betio's Hawkins Field was finally completed, it boasted a 6,450ft by 300ft runway, parking spaces for 72 heavy bombers, hardstands for 100 fighters, plus service facilities. Mullinix Field on Tarawa's nearby Buota Island was completed with a 7,050ft by 200ft runway and a 4,000ft by 150ft runway, both constructed of compacted coral. Mullinix Field could host 76 heavy bombers in dispersed locations. The Seabees' construction of O'Hare Field at Apamama proceeded even slower. O'Hare would not be operational until January 1944 but would eventually boast an 8,000ft coral runway, dispersal capacity for 72 heavy bombers, and modest maintenance equipment. The Seventh Air Force's new Gilberts airfields allowed the Seventh Air Force to advance its heavy bomber, fighter, and dive-bomber squadrons forward from Canton, Funafuti, and Nukufetau, allowing full bomb loads for the first time. Defending the captured Gilberts airfields was the USMC 2nd Defense Battalion.

OPPOSITE THE SEVENTH AIR FORCE ADVANCE IN THE CENTRAL PACIFIC

A Curtiss P-40N Warhawk prepares to launch off escort carrier USS *Breton* (CVE-23), December 10, 1943. On a January 26, 1944 escort mission, P-40s of the 45th Fighter Squadron shot down a confirmed ten A6M Zero fighters and two more probables over Maloelap at no cost to themselves, while their sister P-39s also scored several kills. (Navsource)

On December 1, escort carrier USS *Breton* (CVE-23) departed Oahu carrying 13 P-40Ns to augment the 46th Fighter Squadron. Escort carrier USS *Nassau* (CVE-16) followed on December 3, carrying P-39Qs for the 72nd and 46th Fighter Squadrons. *Nassau* then stopped by Canton to pick up the A-24 Banshees of the 531st Fighter-Bomber Squadron. On December 14 *Nassau* approached Makin Atoll and successfully launched the 72nd Fighter Squadron's P-39s to Makin via catapult. That same day *Breton* launched her 13 P-40Ns to reinforce Canton.

Seventh Air Force raids against the Marshalls began in December 1943. The recent capture of the Gilberts now allowed the Seventh to engage its fighters and light and medium bombers offensively for the first time. These would strike the shorter-range targets, particularly Mille and Jaluit, freeing the B-24s to focus only on the longest range targets. This was not the only advantage of the new forward bases to the heavy bombers. Their closer proximity to heavy bomber targets also reduced the B-24s' average round-trip mission time from 13.7 hours in December to 9.6 hours in February. This allowed heavier bomb loads and more frequent missions, while reducing crew fatigue. The advantages paid off, as the B-24s flew 365 sorties from their bases at Canton and the Ellices in December 1943, focusing on Mille and Maloelap.

The three VII Fighter Command squadrons based on Makin would also directly participate in Operation *Flintlock*. These were the 45th Fighter Squadron (flying P-40Ns), and the 46th and 72nd Fighter Squadrons (both flying P-39s). Their primary objective was to suppress Japanese airfields within range of Kwajalein. However, seemingly the only Marshalls base within range of the P-39s was Mille. On December 18, 1943 the Seventh Air Force launched its first offensive fighter mission of the war when six P-39s out of Makin struck Mille at dawn, destroying six parked aircraft for no loss.

Hours later, 13 P-39s of the 72nd and 46th escorted twelve 531st A-24s in a second Mille strike. On the strike's return a single P-39 went down with engine trouble 65 miles from Makin. The Navy PBY Catalina that attempted to rescue the drifting pilot was itself destroyed when it landed in heavy seas. The PBY's crew ultimately survived in a life raft but the drifting P-39 pilot disappeared as the two parties attempted to reach each other. This first unsuccessful rescue attempt by a Dumbo SAR flight nevertheless heralded the bravery and dedication the SAR crews would display throughout the war.

The Japanese retaliated that night with their own air raid against Makin. The following day, December 19, ten belly tank-equipped P-39s struck Mille again. This time the Japanese were ready with airborne Zeros and heavy anti-aircraft fire. The P-39s destroyed three aircraft on the ground and one Zero in the air but lost two of their own.

VII Fighter Command raids against Japanese islands continued without interruption in preparation for *Flintlock*. Although no two fighter-bomber raids were alike, it is worth examining a ten-day period of Makin-based fighter raids in some detail.

On January 17, 1944, P-40N Warhawks of the 45th Fighter Squadron, each carrying two 500lb bombs on wing racks and a 75-gallon belly tank, took off from Makin and joined a mixed strike of A-24s and P-39s en route to hit Mili. The P-40s flew high cover at 16,000ft, while the P-39s roared in low to strafe Japanese positions ahead of the A-24s. Mili anti-aircraft fire was surprisingly intense, the worst the Americans had seen there in weeks. Two P-39s and one pilot were lost, with the second pilot picked up after he bailed out 90nm from Makin.

The following day, January 18, VII Fighter Command launched a strike against the more distant Jaluit Atoll, some 300nm northwest of Makin, ruling out P-39s. The P-40s of the 45th Fighter Squadron and A-24s of the 531st Fighter-Bomber Squadron targeted Jaluit's seaplane base and any vessels anchored in Jaluit's harbor. The P-40s dove on Jaluit from 10,000ft, released their bombs at 3,000ft, and strafed the island. The 25 A-24s followed with their own dive-bomb runs against an oil storage facility. They scored several hits but lost two A-24s to intense anti-aircraft fire. One two-man crew was lost, but the second crew bailed out into the sea ten miles off Jaluit. Makin immediately scrambled P-39 fighters mounting a new 150-gallon "bathtub" external tank. The P-39s set up CAP relays over the downed crewmen and others escorted a PBY Catalina to a successful rescue.

Then on January 20 the 45th Fighter Squadron bombed and strafed Mili again, followed by Jaluit on January 21. After hitting Mili, a P-40 pilot was forced to bail out 75 miles from Makin, but was picked up by a PBY the next day. The fighter pilots' praise for the skill and dedication of the USN Dumbo crews continued to grow.

On January 25, the 41st Bomb Group requested assistance on a search-and-rescue mission for a downed B-25 north of Arno Atoll. Relays totaling 15 P-40s of the 45th Squadron and four P-39s of the 46th Squadron covered the Dumbo for a successful rescue. At 700 miles round-trip it had been the longest fighter mission so far, bringing the fighters within 80nm of Maloelap Atoll. At Maloelap's Taroa Island was a formidable fighter base whose Zeros had already shot down 15 unescorted B-24s and B-25s and damaged 100 other bombers since the campaign began.

Douglas A-24B Banshee dive-bombers at Makin, December 1943. As a ground-based attack aircraft, the two-man, single-engine A-24 removed the SBD's carrier equipment, primarily the arrestor hook and the solid tail wheel, which the USAAF replaced with a pneumatic tire. (Public Domain)

Inspired by the January 25 mission, VII Fighter Command officers brainstormed how to finally hit Taroa with fighters. A delicate plan was developed that would allow fuel-laden and very carefully flown P-40s from the 45th Squadron to rendezvous with a return-bound B-25 raid 25nm south of Taroa and fight for exactly five minutes. The shorter-ranged P-39s of the 72nd Squadron would conduct CAPs over Mili and help escort the final leg home.

The following day, January 26, nine B-25s of the 47th Bomb Squadron staged through Makin to hit Taroa. Following at a precise distance behind the B-25s were Major Harry Thompson's 12 P-40Ns. Upon reaching Taroa the nine B-25s received the usual fierce reception from Japanese flak and 15 scrambled A6Ms of the 252nd Kokutai. Two B-25s went down, with the A6Ms relentlessly attacking the fleeing B-25s. Flying at 8,000ft, the 12 P-40s dove down to ambush the shocked A6Ms, who had never expected US fighters just off Taroa. The 45th Squadron claimed ten Zeros shot down and two damaged, although Japanese sources only admit to four. The 72nd Squadron P-39s met the returning B-25s and P-40s just off Mili and finished the escort home. No US fighters were lost in the nearly 5-hour combat mission that had covered 800nm. Nimitz, Hale, and a grateful VII Bomber Command skipper Major-General Truman Landon all wired VII Fighter Command their praise of the mission. When the next escorted B-25 mission was attempted, this time against Wotje and Maloelap, it was discovered the Japanese had withdrawn their fighters.

By now Operation *Flintlock*, the invasion of Kwajalein and Majuro, loomed just a week away. D-Day was scheduled for January 31, 1944. The Central Pacific Force's *Flintlock* order of battle largely resembled *Galvanic*. The Fast Carrier Task Force – now designated TF-58 and commanded by Vice Admiral Marc Mitscher – comprised ten fast carriers, 579 carrier aircraft, six fast battleships, ten cruisers, and 29 destroyers. Rear Admiral Richmond K. Turner's Joint Expeditionary Force (TF-51) included 297 ships and transported 54,000 marines and soldiers. Within TF-51 was Turner's Southern Attack Force (TF-53) assigned to assault the main island of Kwajalein, and Rear Admiral Richard L. Conolly's Northern Attack Force (TF-52), which would invade Kwajalein's Roi-Namur Island.

US airpower for *Flintlock* would be substantial. The ten TF-58 fast carriers and six escort carriers of TF-51 combined to give a total of 744 single-engine carrier aircraft. The Seventh

A reconnaissance photo of Kwajalein, January 1944. Kwajalein Atoll had multiple large airstrips, and was the headquarters of the IJN Sixth Fleet, the Japanese submarine force. The decision to invade Kwajalein near the center of the Marshalls was a bold decision by Nimitz. (NHHC 80-G-213594)

Air Force provided an additional 199 aircraft available for combat. These comprised 61 B-24s, as well as 42 B-25s, 22 A-24s, 48 P-39s, and 26 P-40s.

In preparation for D-Day, B-24s dumped 200 tons of bombs on Kwajalein in January 1944, while also striking Wotje and Maloelap heavily. Meanwhile US carrier aircraft began attacking the Marshalls on January 27, 1944. By January 31, no Japanese aircraft remained in the Marshalls.

The 4th Marine Division and 7th Infantry Division landed at Kwajalein and Roi-Namur on January 31, 1944. Compared to Tarawa, resistance was relatively light. To cover the ongoing Kwajalein battle, relays of Makin-based P-40s and P-39s flew daily dawn-till-dusk CAPs over Mille. No Japanese fighter resistance was encountered. In stark contrast to Tarawa, resistance at Kwajalein proved relatively light. The atoll was secured on February 6, with the Americans having lost 348 killed in action.

A desultory raid by six Emily flying boats out of Saipan staged through Ponape and hit Roi-Namur at 0230hrs, February 12. The raid detonated a US supply dump, destroying 80 percent of all ammunition, food, and supplies on the island, and killing 25 Americans. The need for a US night interception capability had never been more apparent.

That same day Makin-based P-39s and A-24s conducted an uneventful raid against Mili. This proved the last mission for the 46th and 72nd Fighter Squadrons, which were shipped via escort carrier back to Oahu.

Now only the P-40s of 45th Squadron remained. They dive-bombed Jaluit on February 16. Noticing a 150ft vessel off Emidji Island, the 45th Squadron refueled and rearmed back at Makin before returning a second time that day. The P-40s scored several hits or near-misses on the Japanese ship, but two fighters were knocked down by intense anti-aircraft fire.

Operation *Catchpole* was slated to invade Eniwetok Atoll on February 17. As usual the Seventh Air Force's supporting mission was to neutralize Japanese airbases within striking distance of the invasion site. The primary targets for the bombers would be Ponape and Kusaie in the eastern Carolines.

Kusaie was in the easternmost of the Carolines and had a small harbor and an airfield under construction.

The late-war skipper of VII Fighter Command, Ernest "Mickey" Moore, photographed as a Major-General. Moore was forbidden by his superiors from flying all the way to Japan, but he insisted on flying the first 200 miles with them in his own P-51. (090217-F-JZ032-298 Media Defense)

B-24s first attacked Kusaie on February 17, then hit the island again on February 20 and February 22. The heaviest raid was on February 24, when B-24s dropped 15 tons of bombs and set the entire waterfront ablaze. This fourth raid completed the virtual destruction of Kusaie as a military base.

More important than Kusaie was Ponape, the largest target the Seventh Air Force had yet attacked. Ponape boasted a medium-sized airfield, a second airfield under construction, and a port large enough to accommodate six medium vessels and many smaller ones. Although Ponape was just 400 miles from Eniwetok it was 1,085 miles from the forward base at Tarawa, requiring a 2,200-mile round trip. B-24s hit Ponape for the first time on February 14. In four raids over the next several weeks the installations at Ponape were largely demolished.

Meanwhile, the 45th Fighter Squadron continued its own raids out of Makin. During a February 22 raid on Mili, the 45th experimented with a single P-40N jury-rigged with two M1 "bazooka" rocket launchers. However, the experiment was judged a failure, as one bazooka failed to ignite while the other apparently missed the target entirely. The same raid also saw

A B-24 takes off from Eniwetok, April 1944. The Americans completed both a fighter strip and a bomber strip at Eniwetok Atoll's Engebi Island; collectively they were known as Wigley Field. A second fighter strip on the islet of Eniwetok was named Stickell Field, while nearby Parry Island hosted a small seaplane base. (NHHC 80-G-251484)

another experiment, as the P-40s dropped their 500lb bombs from 8,000ft. This tactic also failed.

According to Second Lieutenant Herb Henderson, a P-40N pilot in the 45th Squadron: "The Baker and Marshall Island campaigns were excellent training for the long overwater flights that were [later] required at Iwo. They sure taught us to live 'camping out.' Since all of our flying was over water, we learned to trust our compass and other sparse navigation equipment. The Marshalls provided the advanced training we needed to improve our skills in the dive-bombing and strafing of targets."

During the Marshall Islands campaign, the Seventh Air Force had hit Japanese targets on 12 different islands in the Carolines, Gilberts, and Marshalls, dropping 2,812 tons of bombs on the Japanese in 2,897 effective sorties. US forces had managed to partially neutralize Japanese airpower. After each airfield attack the Japanese had urgently tried to keep at least one runway operational through hasty repairs. However, after January 30, 1944, the Seventh Air Force encountered no aerial interception over the Marshalls. Japanese anti-aircraft fire had been intense at the beginning of the Marshalls campaign but fell off rapidly to hoard limited ammunition. Virtually all facilities at Mille, Jaluit, Waloelap, Kusaie, and Ponape had been badly damaged or destroyed, with numerous ammunition magazines obliterated by bomb hits. The Japanese garrisons continued to defend themselves but were never again of any military value.

Operation *Catchpole* successfully concluded in March 1944. The VII Fighter Command then returned to Hawaii, having gained valuable combat experience. During the Gilberts and Marshalls campaigns, the 45th, 46th, and 72nd Fighter Squadrons had flown over 1,100 sorties, including escort, dive-bombing, and strafing missions, as well as the usual fighter sweeps and defensive patrols.

The following month, Brigadier-General Ernest "Mickey" Moore was named the new commander of VII Fighter Command. The "Sun Setters" now had two full fighter groups – the 15th and the 318th, each with four fighter squadrons. Immediately after the change in command the VII Fighter Command was assigned a third Fighter Group, the 21st. The 15th and 318th Groups each transferred a fighter squadron to the new 21st Group.

After entering the war disastrously at Pearl Harbor, the Seventh Air Force was slowly beginning to redeem itself. Between December 1941 to March 1, 1944 the Seventh Air Force

P-39Q Airacobras of the 46th Fighter Squadron line the runway at Makin's Starmann Field, December 1943. Initial airfield construction at Makin was plagued by the swampy terrain. After the war Starmann Field would become the civilian Butaritari Atoll Airport. (USAF)

had flown 4,142 sorties, dropped 3,326 tons of bombs, claimed 110 enemy kills in aerial combat, and admitted to losing 60 Seventh Air Force planes to air-to-air combat.

By now the P-47 and P-38 were arriving in theater to replace the VII Fighter Command's aging P-40s and P-39s. The 15th Fighter Group transitioned to P-47Ds during summer 1944. Meanwhile the 21st Fighter Group, comprising the 46th, 72nd, and 531st Squadrons, flew P-39 Airacobras until midsummer 1944 when they transitioned to P-38L Lightnings.

Neutralizing the Caroline Islands, March 1944–August 1944

One of the primary US planning assumptions for the Central Pacific offensive had been the occupation of Truk, the IJN's major forward Pacific anchorage. Truk, a large lagoon surrounded by mountainous islands, had been widely assumed to be a veritable fortress. But the Fast Carrier Task Force's February 15–17, 1944 raid against Truk had found the atoll surprisingly weak in both defenses and shipping, as overwhelming US carrier airpower easily achieved temporary air supremacy over the base. US planners suddenly decided that Truk could be bypassed. Despite the heavy damage US carrier air had inflicted to Truk's immediate effectiveness as an airbase, it was well understood that airfield damage was temporary. Repairing cratered airstrips could be done literally overnight, while only a few days was required to rebuild light structures and fly in Japanese aerial reinforcement. As the US offensive proceeded through the Central Pacific, near-daily bombing would be required to keep Truk safely neutralized in the American rear. The fast carriers were too valuable and vulnerable for this mission, and so the job fell by default to the B-24 groups of the VII Bomber Command. This would be the primary task of the Seventh's heavy bombardment groups between March 15 and September 15, 1944. In fact the Seventh worked in concert with the Thirteenth Air Force, with the Seventh striking from the Central Pacific theater and the Thirteenth from the South-West Pacific – this was one of the few areas before autumn 1944 that saw the simultaneous and coordinated attention of both MacArthur's command and of Spruance's.

These missions were particularly dangerous. They involved extremely long-distance flights over water, without the security of emergency airfields or fighter escort. When not over the target, the long tediousness and banality of the flights threatened to dull any crew's attention and proficiency.

US planners understood they needed to pre-emptively interdict the expected Japanese aerial reinforcements prior to the planned June 1944 invasion of the Marianas. Japanese air strength was expected to flow to the Marianas via three established air routes. The first was from the Home Islands through Marcus and then Wake Island. The second possible route was from the Home Islands via the Bonins; from there Japanese air strength could either

Truk under attack by US carrier aircraft in early 1944. Truk was the headquarters of the IJN Fourth Fleet and boasted four airfields and a petroleum storage capacity of 77,200 tons but was never as formidably defended as US planners imagined. (US Navy)

Seventh Air Force B-24D Liberators bomb Truk, August 28, 1944

The 253rd Kokutai has scrambled several A6M Zero fighters to intercept the unescorted B-24s raiding Truk, but for the moment the Liberators' defensive armament is keeping them at bay. These B-24 crewmen will never receive anywhere near the fame or press that their compatriots do over Germany or Japan. They are just performing a grinding, methodical, and thankless job, despite the inherent danger involved. These sorts of operation were suppression or harassment raids to keep Truk neutralized as a Japanese air base, and therefore occurred on a daily to weekly basis over the last year of the war.

For decades leading up to the Pacific War, US planners had long assumed that the Japanese forward naval headquarters at Truk, in the Caroline Islands, was essentially Japan's "Pearl Harbor" – that is, highly fortified with anchored warships; heavily-armed, dug-in troops; large numbers of permanently-deployed, land-based aircraft (particularly long-ranged bombers that could far outrange US carriers); and a sophisticated early warning system comprising scores of patrol boats and submarines deployed hundreds of miles out to sea. So taken were the Americans with the Truk legend they had largely produced only in their minds, they took to calling Truk, "The Japanese Gibraltar." One US carrier pilot, upon hearing they were about to hit Truk for the first time, blurted out only half-sarcastically that he would rather just bail out of the briefing room. To be fair, the Japanese had spent virtually the entire 1930s refusing to allow almost any formal visitor anywhere near the island Mandates, suggesting that the Japanese were in fact illegally fortifying the Mandates against international agreement – ironically they were not, at least not yet. In fact Truk was a classic mirror-image job the Americans had misrepresented to themselves. Truk was well fortified for a Japanese Central Pacific atoll, but it was never as well-defended or vital to Japanese strategy as Pearl Harbor was for the Americans.

launch direct attacks against the US amphibious force, or could stage through Truk in a shuttle bombing operation. The third potential route was through Yap and Woleai in the western Carolines and thence to Truk, with aircraft funneled from either the Philippines or the Netherlands East Indies. All three air routes employed Truk as a primary feature. Major facilities at Truk were located on the islands of Param, Moen, Eten, and Dublon. However, only about 40 anti-aircraft guns protected Truk by spring 1944. None were radar-directed, although the atoll's air search radar allowed some warning against potential airstrikes.

The 30th Bomb Group launched the first Seventh Air Force strike against Truk on March 14, 1944, staging through Kwajalein from the Gilberts. After being refueled and loaded with bombs, 22 total B-24s departed Kwajalein at 2200hrs. Ultimately 13 of 22 B-24s penetrated a tropical storm to bomb Truk in darkness, arriving at 0300hrs, March 15. After a few minutes of surprise, Truk was blacked out and searchlights and moderate flak began to pierce the air. Three Japanese night fighters made ineffective attacks. No B-24s were lost on this first mission. Despite the mission's success, it was decided to move the B-24s to Kwajalein and prepare Eniwetok as a staging base before resuming Truk raids. With Truk temporarily off the table, the following two weeks would see the B-24s hit Wake, Ponape, and Mille-Maloelap twice each.

However, Mitscher's Fast Carrier Task Force was scheduled to hit the Palaus on March 30 and the Seventh Air Force was tasked with softening up Truk ahead of time. The Seventh launched its second Truk strike the afternoon of March 28. Twenty-one B-24s headed for the target, with 17 reaching Truk at 2100hrs after four B-24s aborted. Cloud cover frustrated the strike, although anti-aircraft fire was ineffective and Japanese fighters stayed on the ground. Although no B-24s were lost, bombing results were poor.

The first daylight bombing mission was made on March 29, 1944 by the Seventh's 307th Bomb Group. Two squadrons totaling 24 B-24s had staged through Torokina from Munda the previous day, with 20 Liberators reaching Truk. At least 15 fighters met the B-24s ten minutes before the target, with more fighters waiting below. Intense flak from land batteries and three destroyers greeted the B-24s, flying at 17,000ft altitude.

A reported 75 aerial attacks were made by Zeros and Tonys after the B-24s' attack run, including dropping phosphorus bombs among the US formation. Two B-24s and 21 airmen would be lost, but post-strike photo reconnaissance would indicate most of 49 parked aircraft destroyed.

The Seventh launched its fourth Truk strike the night of March 29/30, 1944. These strikes were launched in conjunction with the Thirteenth Air Force's 868th Squadron, which heckled Dublon with fragmentation clusters overnight, and Mitscher's Fast Carrier Task Force, which hit the Palaus early on March 30. The night of March 30 some 21 B-24s of the 11th Bombing Group hit Truk with 42 tons of 100lb bombs. The following night the 30th Bomb Group hit Truk with 14 B-24s carrying 500lb bombs.

The Seventh would attack Truk three more times during this blitz, on the nights of April 2/3, April 3/4, and finally the largest strike yet, 24 Liberators on the night of April 6/7. April missions continued, with Seventh Air Force squadrons flying in rotation. By the end of April the Seventh had dropped 734 tons of bombs against Truk in 329 sorties, losing five B-24s. On April 28/29 they received considerable assistance from Mitscher's fast carriers, which dropped 748 tons of bombs in 2,200 sorties against Truk, destroying 93 Japanese planes and virtually annihilating Japanese airpower at Truk, at least for the moment.

Although Truk was the main focus, the VII Bomber Command also hit other targets in the air route system. Between March and May 1944 the Seventh Air Force launched 12 total strikes against Wake Island, accumulating 204 total B-24 sorties. Hale additionally experimented with mixed strikes of B-24s, B-25s, F6Fs, F4Us, and SBDs against Jaluit on May 14/15, Wotje on May 21, and Ponape on May 27/28. B-25s of the 41st Bomb Group also kept up neutralization raids against bypassed outposts in the Marshalls.

Wake Island under attack by Seventh Air Force B-24s in March 1944. Wake was initially garrisoned by the IJN 65th Guard Force and the 13th Independent Mixed Regiment. Wake was bombarded by sea and by air throughout the war but ultimately bypassed by the Americans. (NHHC 80-G-220349)

By now VII Bomber Command was preparing to support the upcoming Operation *Forager*, the invasion of the Marianas. On June 6, B-24s staged a photo-bombing mission over Guam, then hit Truk five nights in a row between June 8 and June 12. Twenty-seven B-24s of the 11th Bomb Group hit Truk in daylight on June 13, followed by another night attack on June 14. By June 19 the IJN Combined Fleet was approaching Saipan and B-24s from Kwajalein responded by hammering Truk five days in a row.

June 1944 was the peak of the Truk raids, with VII Bomber Command dropping 566 tons of bombs against the atoll. By July 1, VII Bomber Command launched four raids a week against Truk, which dropped to two per week by August 1. These seemingly mundane yet vital Truk suppression raids would continue on a similar pattern through the end of the war.

The Mariana Islands operation, June–August 1944

On May 1, 1944 the Pacific command arrangements underwent yet another reorganization. The Shore Based Air Force, Forward Area, was established as a joint task force designated Task Force 59 under the command of Major-General Hale, whose title would be ComAirForward. Hale would be responsible for the operation of all shore-based aircraft in the forward area, including fighters, bombers, air evacuation, and air transport. As ComAirForward, Hale would continue to operate under the command of Vice Admiral Hoover, Commander, Forward Area (ComForArea). Hale's Task Force 59 was headquartered at Kwajalein. Replacing Hale as Seventh Air Force Commander was Brigadier-General Robert Douglas Jr, former commander of VII Fighter Command.

CINCPOA had by now formulated Campaign Plan *Granite II*, which would involve the sequential invasions of the Mariana Islands and Palau Islands. Except for the American territory of Guam, captured by the Japanese in the first days of the war, the Mariana Islands

OPPOSITE SEVENTH AIR FORCE CLOSE AIR SUPPORT TACTICS DEVELOPED DURING THE MARIANA ISLANDS CAMPAIGN

Japanese trenches were typically in a zigzag pattern parallel to the beach, resulting in the Seventh Air Force fighters making their strafing runs perpendicular to the beach. The fighters would begin their strafing runs at an altitude of 4,000ft and make their strafing dives at a 60-degree angle. During the strafing run, the fighters fired their guns in short bursts. The fighters would pull out of their strafing dive at an altitude of 1,000ft. Artillery shells could fly as high as 4,000ft so it was important that artillery barrages were suspended during the US fighter strafing runs.

If the Japanese target was particularly small, such as a foxhole or a gun emplacement, fighters would first make a "dry run" pass at an altitude of just 200ft to confirm the target, then climb to 2,000ft and begin the usual 60-degree strafing dive.

had been under Japanese control since 1914. The Japanese had built major airfields and naval facilities on the islands of Saipan, Tinian, Rota, and Pagan, but had only belatedly begun to fortify the islands in early 1944. Unlike the previous campaigns' flat, tiny atolls, the Marianas were rugged volcanic islands of substantial size and elevation, allowing large ground forces to defend in depth.

The US invasion of the Marianas was codenamed Operation *Forager* and it would follow the basic pattern introduced at the Gilberts and refined since then. *Forager* would invade three islands in sequence: Saipan, Guam, and Tinian. D-Day for the first target, Saipan, was set for June 15, 1944. Once Saipan's Aslito Field was taken, the 318th Fighter Group, having just converted from P-40s to P-47Ds that June, would be ferried to Saipan to assist in *Forager*, with the 15th and 21st Fighter Groups remaining behind in Hawaii.

Months earlier the IJN had undergone a major reorganization of its Central Pacific command. The IJN Central Pacific Area Fleet was established on March 4, 1944. Its commander was Vice Admiral Chuichi Nagumo, the same admiral who just 27 months earlier had humiliated the Hawaiian Air Force at Pearl Harbor. Subordinated within the Central Pacific Area Fleet was the IJN Fourth Fleet, the newly-established IJN 14th Air Fleet (*Dai-Juyon Koku Kantai*), the cruiser *Isuzu*, the No. 5 Special Base Force, the No. 30 Special Base Force, and the No. 4 Weather Observation Unit. By June 1, 1944, the IJNAF 1st Air Fleet had four Air Flotillas established in the Central Pacific area. These were the 61st Air Flotilla and the 22nd Air Flotilla in the Carolines, the 26th Air Flotilla in the Philippines and northwestern New Guinea, and the 23rd Air Flotilla. Lieutenant-General Hideyoshi Obata's IJA 31st Army garrisoned the entire Marianas, as well as Truk. Its 80,000 troops were divided between numerous islands where they were unable to support each other. Saipan itself was defended by the IJA 43rd Division, the IJA 47th Mixed Independent Brigade, and numerous support units. Total strength came to 25,500 IJA and 6,200 IJN personnel under the command of Lieutenant-General Yoshitsugu Saito.

Spruance's Central Pacific Force, recently re-designated US Fifth Fleet, now reached staggering proportions, ultimately comprising over 500 ships and 300,000 men by June 1944. Vice Admiral Marc Mitscher retained command of the Fast Carrier Task Force (TF-58), which had grown to 15 fast carriers, 896 carrier aircraft, seven fast battleships, 21 cruisers, and 58 destroyers. Newly-promoted Vice Admiral Richmond K. Turner again commanded the overall Joint Amphibious Forces, TF-51, as well as directly commanding TF-51's subordinate Northern Attack Force, TF-52.

The V Amphibious Corps' 2nd and 4th Marine Divisions landed at Saipan on D-Day, June 15, and would secure Saipan's Aslito airfield early on June 20. Ground echelons of the 19th and 73rd Fighter Squadrons would arrive that afternoon, while the 804th Aviation Engineering Battalion and Seabees of the 121st Naval Construction Battalion quickly began repairing Aslito for American use.

The 318th Fighter Group had been assigned to deploy from captured Saipan airfields. At Pearl Harbor, the 318th Group's 19th and 73rd Fighter Squadrons loaded 37 P-47Ds

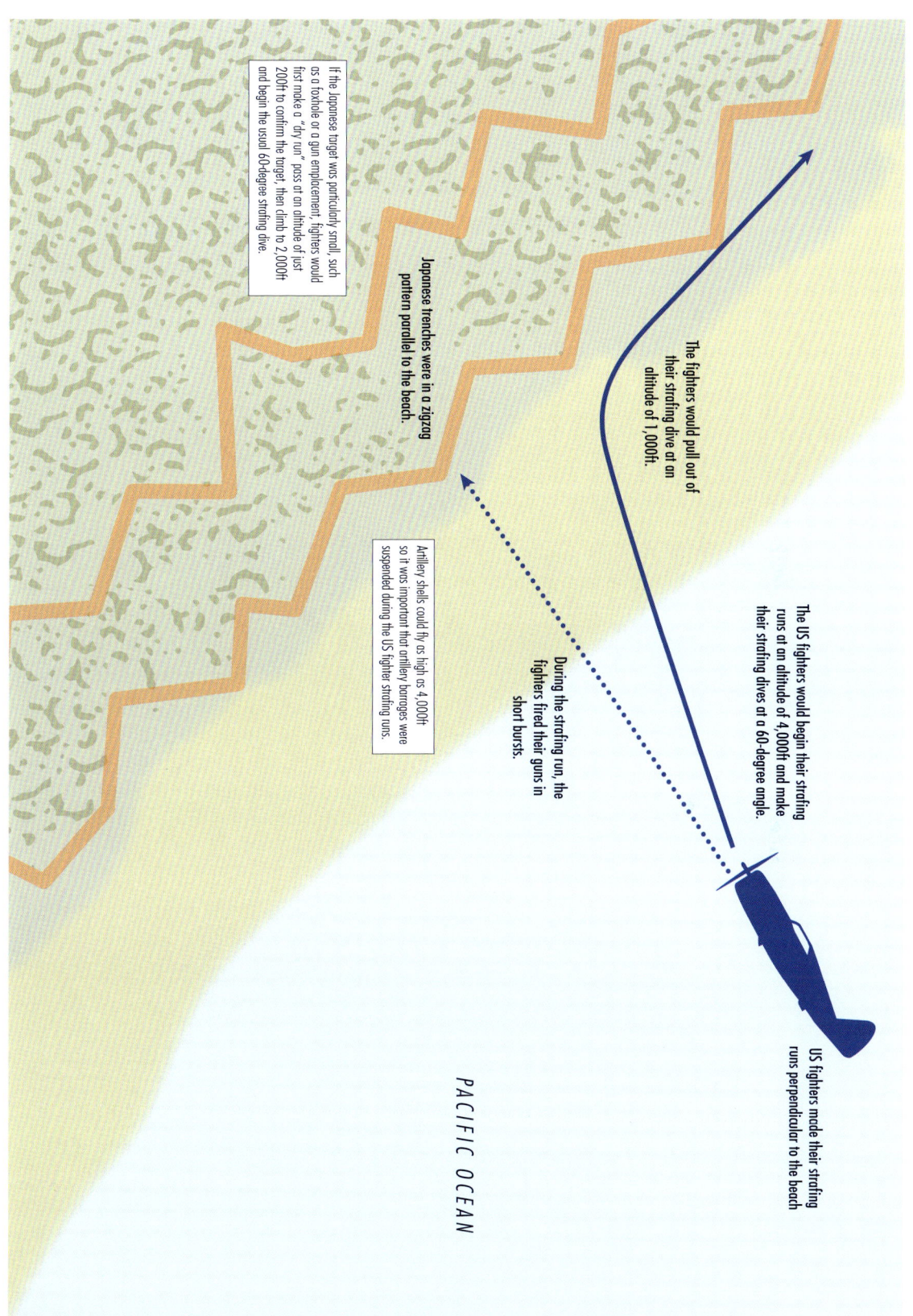

Bombs just miss escort carrier USS *Manila Bay* (CVE-61) on June 23, 1944. *Manila Bay* had been refueling from an oiler off Saipan when four D3A Val dive-bombers appeared suddenly from dead ahead. *Manila Bay* broke free from the oiler as the Vals attacked through heavy anti-aircraft fire before escaping. *Manila Bay* then launched her P-47s to Saipan. (Navsource)

each aboard escort carriers USS *Natoma Bay* (CVE-62) and USS *Manila Bay* (CVE-61) respectively. The two little carriers then departed Pearl Harbor on June 5 to ferry the squadrons to Saipan. They reached Saipan's eastern approaches on June 19, but were ordered to loiter east of Saipan until Spruance's Fifth Fleet had repulsed the approaching IJN carrier fleet. By June 22 the Battle of the Philippine Sea had resolved into a clear American victory and the escort carriers were cleared to steam west and launch their charges.

On June 22, 1944, 318th Group deputy commander Lieutenant-Colonel Charlie Taylor led 25 P-47Ds of the 19th Squadron off *Natoma Bay* (CVE-62). It was Taylor's third escort carrier launch, making him the USAAF's all-time leader. After the P-47Ds landed at Saipan's Aslito Field, eight were immediately fitted with rocket launchers and their flyers sent back aloft on CAS patrol. None had ever seen combat. Upon requesting a target, they were dispatched to Tinian and made repeated strafing and rocket passes at buildings, barges, and a radio tower.

Meanwhile, the *Natoma Bay* had been unable to catapult launch the entire 19th Squadron by evening, and launched the squadron's 12 remaining P-47Ds early on June 23. Both escort carriers then steamed to a refueling location 45nm east, where they were attacked unsuccessfully by four Val dive-bombers, which escaped out of range. *Manila Bay* launched four P-47Ds to fly CAP overhead until the radar screens cleared, which Spruance himself later praised as "commendable initiative." Once the situation had resolved, the four P-47Ds continued on to Saipan.

Manila Bay launched the rest of 73rd Squadron to Saipan the following day, June 24. The establishment of two P-47D squadrons at Aslito allowed the USAAF to take over the air defense role and free the USN's vulnerable carriers for other missions. However, Japanese air raids and artillery fire against Aslito would continue to harass the USAAF ground crews into early July.

Meanwhile, the 6th Night Fighter Squadron, re-equipped with brand-new P-61 Black Widows, also arrived at Aslito on June 24 and immediately commenced night fighter patrol duty. However, a landing accident the night of June 25/26 destroyed two P-61s and killed their crews, leaving just five operational P-61s. Nevertheless, the 6th Night Fighter Squadron scored its first probable kill the night of June 27, and its first confirmed kill on June 30, downing a Betty.

The Marianas campaign was the first time the Seventh Air Force had been employed in the direct support of ground troops. Close Air Support (CAS) of ground troops had been the USAAF's lowest priority before the war. The same was true of naval aviation, meaning wartime CAS doctrine had to be developed on the fly. However, the extreme distances involved in the Central Pacific meant that close air support during the initial assault phase would usually have to come from USN carriers until airfields could be built or captured close enough to mount land-based fighters against the objective.

Since February 1944, Central Pacific amphibious operations had been conducted from a purpose-fitted amphibious command ship (AGC) rather than a battleship. The command ship controlled three dedicated radio nets, each comprising two high frequency (HF) channels and two very high frequency (VHF) channels.

Each radio net was assigned to separate functions. The first circuit, Support Air Request (SAR), was used by ALPs to request close air support missions from the CSA (Commanders, Support Aircraft). The second net, Support Air Direction (SAD), was assigned to aircraft arriving on station to request instructions from the CSA. The third net was dedicated to the new Support Air Observation (SAO). This circuit was used by airborne observers communicating with a ground officer reporting on the tactical situation.

Until command passed to the landing force ashore, all close air support was controlled by the naval assault commander. This was exercised through multiple officers: one or more CSA stationed aboard a flagship; one or more Airborne Coordinators (AC) flying overhead; and multiple Airborne Liaison Parties (ALP) attached to landing force units. Each ALP comprised one USN officer, one USAAF officer, and two USAAF enlisted men.

Northrop P-61 Black Widows defend Saipan, June 30, 1944

The US 6th Night Fighter Squadron, flying Northrop P-61 Black Widows, arrived on Saipan on June 24, 1944, just nine days after the marines' initial landings. They immediately commenced night interceptor patrols, but a landing accident the night of June 25/26 destroyed two P-61s and killed their crews, leaving just five P-61s available. However, a P-61 claimed its first probable the following night, June 27. The 6th Night Fighter Squadron snagged its first confirmed kill by a P-61 the night of June 30, 1944, when it downed a G4M Betty, seen here. The Japanese nevertheless held the initiative until the deployment of new Microwave Early Warning radars linked to SCR–615 and AN/TPS-10 "Li'l Abner" height-finder radars; this new combination on Saipan made US nighttime interception much more effective. The 6th and 548th Night Fighter Squadrons would ultimately shoot down five more Japanese bombers by the time the Saipan raids ended in January 1945. These nighttime raids typically comprised about a dozen Mitsubishi G4M Betty bombers, stretched out about 20 miles apart. The P-61 crews found that if they could down the lead Betty, the others would typically jettison their ordnance and flee for home.

Several months later at Iwo Jima, the USAAF would deploy SCR-527 and SCR-270 radar sets for early warning, and use an AN/TPS-10 for ground control of interceptions. During the height of Japanese heckler raids on Iwo Jima, about two or three Japanese bombers would raid the island each night. The US early warning radar could detect the bombers up to 140 miles out when flying at an altitude between 7,000 and 15,000ft. Around 57 miles out, the AN/TPS-10 ground control operators would vector the P-61s of the 548th and 549th Night Fighter Squadrons to intercept them (the 6th Night Fighter Squadron having been left behind to defend Saipan). Typically the Japanese bombers would begin dropping chaff at a range of 30 miles out, which confused the older metric wave radars, but not the 3cm microwave AN/TPS-10. If the P-61s hadn't shot down or repulsed the Japanese within 10 miles out, they would break off and allow Iwo Jima's anti-aircraft guns to take over. After May 1945, Japanese raids against Iwo Jima fell off sharply, and the 548th and 549th Night Fighter Squadrons were largely redirected to night intruder operations against the Bonins.

Having also debuted in the Marshalls campaign was the new Joint Assault Signal Company (JASCO), a direct response to the Tarawa failures. A JASCO combined USN elements with either an Army or a USMC element and was composed of three sections: naval gunfire control, beach control, and air-ground liaison. The 52-man air-ground liaison section was itself divided into 13 separate Air Liaison Parties (ALP), with one ALP each attached to every divisional, regimental, and battalion headquarters in the landing force.

The P-47s of the 19th and 73rd Squadrons would fly 144 combat sorties by the time Saipan was declared secure on July 9. Now they immediately began flying missions against nearby Tinian, striking Japanese positions with 500lb and 1,000lb bombs, and strafing with their .50cal. machine guns. The 318th Group's last unit, the 333rd Squadron, had been forced to wait in Hawaii for a month while necessary shipping was scraped up. Finally, the 36 P-47Ds of the 333rd Squadron were loaded aboard escort carrier USS *Sargent Bay* (CVE-83). On July 18, 1944, they catapulted off their host and landed at Saipan.

After two weeks of intense air-sea bombardment, Rear Admiral Richard L. Conolly's Southern Attack Force (TF-53) landed the III Amphibious Corps at Guam on W-Day, July 21, 1944. Three days later the 4th Marine Division landed at Tinian on J-Day, July 24, followed by the 2nd Marine Division on July 25. Tinian had also received a heavy softening-up bombardment. The 318th Group's P-47s had been active bombing and strafing enemy positions and marking the landing sites for the assault troops. Tinian was secured against relatively light resistance on August 1, 1944.

The P-47s proved themselves impressively suited to the ground support role, strafing with their eight .50cal. machine guns, dropping bombs, and firing rockets. In late July the P-47s began employing "firebombs" for the first time. These had only recently been developed at Eglin Field, Florida and immediately shipped to Saipan. The firebombs consisted of wing or belly tanks filled with a mixture of diesel oil and gasoline, later changed to a mix of napalm and gasoline (napalm bombs). The firebombs were dropped from an altitude of 50ft after a 2,000ft dive and cleared an area 200ft by 70ft.

US ground crew maintain a 41st Bomb Group B-25 at Betio's Hawkins Field while native islanders look on. The B-25 became famous for field modifications in the South-West Pacific that turned it into a low-level strafing monster. The 41st Bomb Group was the only Seventh Air Force air group flying B-25s throughout the Central Pacific campaign. (Public Domain)

In addition to the full 318th Fighter Group, in late July the 41st Bomb Group (M) had flown in its 48th Bombardment Squadron of B-25s to Saipan and flew CAS until the islands were fully secured. The B-25s flew low-level strafing attacks with machine guns and their 75mm cannon, flying 69 sorties against Tinian during the July 27–31 period and then 91 sorties over Guam between August 3–8. Guam was secured on August 10 against heavy resistance, ending the ground phase of the Marianas campaign. The 48th Squadron's B-25s now returned to Makin to resume its neutralization missions of the Marshalls, Nauru, and Ponape alongside the rest of the 41st Bomb Group. However, the 318th Fighter Group would remain in the Marianas as fighter defense.

The Americans had occupied only the three largest and most important islands in the Marianas – Saipan, Tinian, and Guam, and in their usual fashion expected to use the Seventh Air Force to keep the Marianas' remaining Japanese islands suppressed into impotence.

Philippine Sea diversions, August 1944–January 1945

Since November 1943 the Seventh Air Force had been operating from cramped and primitive facilities carved out of miniscule atolls scarcely larger than anchored aircraft carriers. Saipan though had an area of 40 square miles, seeming tremendous in size compared to the previous atoll bases.

The Americans therefore worked feverishly to develop the Marianas as a major airbase. Although the Marianas' main purpose was to host the B-29s of the XXI Bomber Command, by late August 1944 the 318th Fighter Group was based at Kagman Point Field at Saipan, while the 30th Bomb Group (Heavy) was based at Saipan's Aslito Field, now renamed Isley Field by the Americans. On Guam, Agana airfield would base the 11th Bomb Group (Heavy) by the end of October 1944.

On August 1, 1944 the US Seventh Air Force was stripped of its service functions and formally reorganized into a mobile, tactical air force within the newly-created Army Air Forces, Pacific Ocean Areas (AAFPOA), an umbrella organization encompassing all USAAF assets within Nimitz's Pacific Ocean Areas command. AAFPOA was commanded by Major-General Millard F. Harmon, who was also named deputy commander of the Twentieth Air Force.

The Seventh Air Force's combat groups remained widely scattered and the command set-up remained complex. Administrative control was divided between Seventh Air Force, VII Fighter Command, and 7th Fighter Wing. However, most Seventh Air Force combat units remained subordinated within Task Force 59 (ComAirForward) and later, Task Force 93 (StratAirPOA). VII Fighter Command fighters would be directed by the commander of Task Force 93 in raids against the Nampo Shoto, and by the commander of Task Force 94 (ComForwardArea) when engaged in defense of US-occupied islands, particularly the Marianas.

The general Central Pacific objective between August and December 1944 was the capture, occupation, defense, and development of island bases at Ulithi, southern Palau, and Morotai. By occupying these islands US forces would cut off the remaining Japanese bases in the Marshalls and Carolines, including Truk, while protecting the Marianas and securing a safe route for the invasion of the Philippines.

Lieutenant-General Millard F. Harmon poses in front of an early-model P-51 in January 1944. Harmon's AAFPOA command was largely administrative and logistic, although Nimitz put Harmon in charge of Strategic Air, Pacific Ocean Areas (Task Force 93). On February 26, 1944, a plane carrying Harmon took off from Kwajalein for Pearl Harbor but was never seen again. (Public Domain)

As usual, the Seventh Air Force's mission was the neutralization of Japanese bases in the Central Pacific, the interdiction of Japanese shipping, and air defense of the Americans' own bases. Indeed, the nature of the Americans' island-hopping campaign meant numerous Japanese-held islands were within bomber range of the Marianas airfields. Iwo Jima was just 600 miles to the north, and Truk 600 miles to the southeast. Additional bypassed Japanese bases remained at Wake, Nauru, the Marshalls, and the Carolines. Outside the American advance were Japanese bases at Yap, Palau, Marcus, Pagan and Rota in the Marianas, the Bonin Islands (Chichi Jima and Haha Jima), and the Volcano Islands (Iwo Jima).

The most important Mariana Islands remaining in Japanese hands were Pagan and Rota, which boasted airfields. While most other islands needed only the occasional visit, on Pagan a Japanese garrison of 3,000 men proved quite effective at repairing their runway as fast as it was damaged. Accordingly, from August 1944 through March 1945 the 318th Fighter Group, based on Saipan, would fly 1,578 sorties to keep Pagan suppressed.

P-61 Black Widows of the 6th Night Fighter Squadron at Saipan. The 6th flew its first mission with P-61s the night of June 25, 1944, immediately after arriving at Saipan, and scored its first kill on June 30. The 6th would score two more kills by July 21, 1944. (Public Domain)

Additionally, several islands in the extended Nampo Shoto chain had Japanese airbases, such as Iwo Jima in the Volcano Islands and Haha Jima in the Bonins. Of all the Japanese islands within tactical range of the Marianas, Iwo Jima was particularly concerning as it boasted three airfields and was once photographed basing 175 enemy planes. Therefore, the Seventh Air Force's primary mission in late 1944 was the interdiction of Iwo Jima. The Seventh's first Iwo Jima raid came on August 16, 1944. Nine more missions would be flown over Iwo Jima through August 31. The Seventh Air Force would hit Iwo with 22 more raids in September 1944 and 16 in October.

The IJAAF reorganized a training squadron equipped with obsolete Mitsubishi Ki-21 Sally bombers into the 2nd Hikotai, tasked with raiding the Marianas B-29 bases. The night of November 2, 1944, nine Honshu-based Sallys staged through Iwo Jima and attacked Isley and Kobler Fields, losing three Sallys to flak and P-61s for little gain. Ten more Japanese planes attacked on November 6/7, missing the parked B-29s and losing three to US flak.

Meanwhile, in June 1944 the new B-24-equipped 494th Bomb Group (Heavy) had been assigned to the Seventh Air Force. However, the 494th would be destined for the Palau Island group in MacArthur's South-West Pacific Area of operations. They would be accompanied by the 28th Photo Squadron, which was deployed at Peleliu by early October 1944.

Angaur, in the Palau group and five miles from Peleliu, was ready for heavy bombers on October 21, 1944. Upon arrival the 494th Group's B-24s, despite remaining the administrative responsibility of the Seventh, fell under the SWPA's Fifth Air Force, which was itself subordinated to the US Army Forces Far East command. Angaur thus became the base for the 494th Bomb Group under the operational control of V Bomber Command. During November and December 1944, B-24s of the 494th Bomb Group would pursue the interdiction of Japanese airfields on Babelthaup, Northern Palau group, and in the Philippines.

By November 1944, Seventh Air Force units were stationed within striking distances of all Japan's Central Pacific bases. Farther in the rear, the Seventh Air Force still used airfields at Kwajalein and Eniwetok, as well as Makin in the Gilberts.

A destroyed B-29 Superfortress burning at Isley Field, Saipan, November 27, 1944. The Japanese raids against the Marianas airfields could never be decisive, but they were irritating and, as USAAF chief Hap Arnold pointed out, a B-29 cost three times as much as a B-17. (USAF)

After Iwo Jima, Truk remained VII Bomber Command's second-most important target, and the primary target of its Kwajalein-based B-24s. Between August 1 and October 16, the B-24s of the 11th and 30th Bomb Groups, flying from Kwajalein and staging through Eniwetok, had mounted a total of 499 sorties against Truk in twice-weekly high-altitude daylight raids. The B-24s were intercepted on 18 of 20 missions, but lost only one bomber that crash-landed back at base. Initially, Truk had been able to scramble 12 to 14 fighters against each August strike, but in September this number declined to around eight fighters and then to just three or four fighters per raid in October. Wotje, Jaluit, Mille, and Wake still received occasional attention as the targets for B-24 training raids. The B-25s of the 41st Bomb Group (M) maintained their own neutralization raids against Nauru and Ponape, flying from Makin and Engebi respectively.

On November 20, 1944 a US convoy near Truk was attacked twice in four hours by Japanese aircraft. In response, 24 Liberators hit Truk in force on November 22. They were escorted for the first time by 25 P-38L Lightnings of the 318th Group, who had recently received the new fighter specifically for Truk escort. Eight A6Ms rose to intercept, and four were shot down by the P-38s. The VII Bomber Command would ultimately drop nearly 1,000 tons of bombs on Truk during the August–December 1944 period. Enough damage was consistently inflicted to airfields and other military installations to keep Truk's forces off balance.

On November 27, 1944, two G4M Betty bombers swooped in low over Saipan, destroying one B-29 and damaging eleven. Shortly afterwards the 252 Kokutai mounted a near suicide mission against the Marianas. Twelve bomb-armed A6M Zeros executed a one-way, wave-top attack against Saipan by staging through Iwo Jima. One Zero was lost to operational causes but the remaining 11 achieved complete surprise, destroying three B-39s and damaging two more. Four P-47s scrambled to defend the base. The P-47s shot down four Zeros, while anti-aircraft fire claimed six more. The final Zero boldly landed at Isley Field, whereupon its pilot dismounted and drew a pistol before being shot to death by US infantry. Unfortunately for the Americans, one P-47 had been lost to friendly anti-aircraft fire. The following night, six G4M Bettys bombed Isley from high altitude, but with little success.

To reinforce US defenses, Vice Admiral Hoover stationed two destroyers 100 miles northwest of Saipan as early warning radar pickets. These gave about 25 minutes' notice of an incoming Japanese raid. Fighters available to scramble included the 318th Fighter Group's P-47s and the 6th Night Fighter Squadron's P-61s. Saipan was additionally defended by eight US Army anti-aircraft battalions and two searchlight battalions. The harassment raids nevertheless proved difficult to stop; the Seventh Air Force had already struck Iwo Jima 30 times in November.

On December 7 the Japanese struck Isley with a combined force of G4M and Ki-67 bombers, destroying three B-29s at heavy loss to themselves. CINCPOA now directed a choreographed air-sea attack against Iwo Jima. On December 8, the Seventh Air Force hit Iwo with a fighter sweep of 28 P-38s, followed by 102 B-24s. In between, the XXI Bomber Command struck Iwo with 62 B-29s. Finally, the heavy cruisers *Chester*, *Pensacola*, and *Salt Lake City*, plus six destroyers, shelled Iwo for over an hour. The little island had absorbed 814 tons of bombs, 1,500 8in. shells, and 5,334 5in. shells in barely half a day. Later photoreconnaissance revealed that little real damage had been done, but the Saipan raids ended for the moment.

Chester, *Pensacola*, *Salt Lake City*, and five destroyers returned to shell Iwo on December 24, again coordinated with a B-24 strike. This bombardment proved particularly ineffective, as the following Christmas night, December 25/26, the Japanese mounted their single largest attack on Saipan. Some 25 bombers hit Isley from high and low altitudes in the dark, destroying one B-29 and damaging three more. Finally, on January 2, 1945 the Japanese launched their last raid against Saipan, losing one plane to a P-61. Since August 1944 the Japanese had dispatched 80 to 100 sorties against the B-29s' Marianas bases, mostly at night, losing 37 planes in the process. Total US losses to the Japanese harassment raids had been eleven B-29s destroyed and 43 damaged, a profitable exchange for the Japanese. Nevertheless, it had been the Seventh Air Force's continual presence over Iwo Jima the previous five months that kept the B-29 force from suffering far greater damage.

P-47D Thunderbolts of the 318th Fighter Group take off from Saipan's East Field, October 1944. US aviation engineers on Saipan shipped in drums of hardened asphalt and then used an abandoned sugar boiler to produce a melting plant. Several hundred tons of asphalt was then laid over a crushed coral base 12–18 inches deep to build Saipan's airstrips. (USAF)

Throughout late 1944 the Seventh had ranged over the Marshalls, Carolines, Marianas, Bonin, and Volcano Islands, hammering Iwo Jima the hardest. The Seventh Air Force had dropped 7,063 tons of ordnance against Japanese targets in 4,525 effective sorties. Of these, Iwo Jima received over 3,000 tons from 1,466 sorties. The Seventh had flown 79 missions against Iwo in December alone.

Even after the US occupation of the Marianas, the B-24s remained the Seventh's primary offensive weapon for hitting Japanese targets, particularly Truk, Iwo Jima, Marcus, and the Bonin Islands. December 1944 also saw the Seventh's heavy bomber force peak in strength, with 151 B-24s available for the continued attacks against the Philippines, Iwo Jima, and Truk.

The next coordinated bombardment of Iwo Jima came on January 25. Seventh Air Force B-24s and P-38s pounded Iwo for three hours. The USN contributed battleship *Indiana*, cruisers *Chester*, *Pensacola*, and *Salt Lake City*, and the usual destroyer escort. Over the next two hours Iwo Jima endured the ministrations of 203 16in. and 1,354 8in. shells. Again the bombardment did little real damage, but the Japanese had already decided to call off further Saipan raids.

The Iwo Jima operation, February–March 1945

Back on October 3, 1944, the US Joint Chiefs of Staff had authorized the sequential invasions of Luzon, Iwo Jima, and Okinawa. Although Seventh Air Force was largely irrelevant to the Luzon operation, it would be crucial for the latter two invasions. Spruance planned to use Iwo Jima as a fighter base to support his carriers. This idea fell in line with USAAF brass, who in early 1944 had hoped to base five P-51 fighter groups there to escort the planned B-29 raids against the Home Islands. Okinawa was much larger and closer to Japan and boasted several good anchorages. If captured by the Americans it would make an ideal staging base not just for major air-sea raids against the Home Islands, but for a potential amphibious invasion of Japan itself.

However, delays in airfield construction on Leyte would push back the entire timetable of US operations. In January 1945 the invasion of Iwo Jima, codenamed Operation *Detachment*, was delayed to February 19, while the invasion of Okinawa, Operation *Iceberg*, was pushed back to April 1.

B-24 Liberators shortly after bombing Iwo Jima, December 15, 1944. Between August 10, 1944 and February 15, 1945, VII Bomber Command B-24s alone would dump 5,582 tons of ordnance on Iwo Jima. The B-24s never destroyed Iwo as an airbase, but did keep it suppressed enough to never mount a major air campaign against the Marianas. (Public Domain)

During this period the Seventh Air Force was tasked with three missions. The first was the continued interdiction of outflanked or bypassed Japanese bases. In order of priority, these were: Iwo Jima; Chichi Jima; Haha Jima; Marcus; Truk; the Japanese-held part of Palau (Babelthaup); and the Japanese-held Marianas (Pagan and Rota Islands). The Seventh's second mission was supporting Operation *Detachment*, the amphibious invasion of Iwo Jima. The Seventh's third mission (through the 494th Bomb Group) was to continue supporting the Philippines campaign by neutralizing Japanese bases located in Luzon, Mindanao, Negros, Cebu, Mactan, and Corregidor. Meanwhile, the Marianas would continue to be further developed as a major base.

Back in November 1944, Major-General Haywood Hansell's Marianas-based B-29 Superfortresses – the XXI Bomber Command – had begun their strategic bombing raids against the Home Islands. What USAAF brass had initially expected to be a war-winning turn of

Task Force 94 aircraft and US Navy's Cruiser Division Five bombard Iwo Jima, December 8, 1944

EVENTS

1. Twenty-eight P-38 Lightnings of the 318th Fighter Group take off from Saipan at 0628hrs, December 8 to conduct a coordinated fighter sweep of Iwo Jima. They are organized into seven flights — Violet 1 through Violet 7 — and are navigationally led to the target by three B-29 escorts. The objective is to clear Iwo Jima of any fighter resistance before the later planned raids by B-29s and B-24s.

2. At 0945hrs the 318th Fighter Group P-38s and their three B-29 escorts arrive five miles south of Iwo Jima at an altitude of 18,000ft. The plan is for flights Violet 1, Violet 2, and Violet 3 to make a sweep around the west side of Iwo Jima, while Violet 4, Violet 5, and Violet 6 sweep around the east side of Iwo Jima. Violet 7 will remain with the three B-29 escorts five miles south of Iwo Jima. However, upon arriving at the target it is discovered that Iwo Jima is completely obscured by overcast from an altitude of 1,000ft up to 8,000ft.

3. Almost immediately, three A6M Zekes are sighted to the immediate west at 20,000ft. They are driven off and down through the overcast by the four P-38s of Violet 3, with one A6M visibly damaged by P-38 fire. Violet 3 climbs back to 16,000ft.

4. Violet 4 returns to the B-29s five miles south of Iwo Jima and spies an approaching A6M through the overcast, which is shot down by Violet 4-1.

EVENTS

5. Violet 5 makes a complete search of the area from an altitude between 18,000ft and 12,000ft but ascertains little information through the overcast.

6. Violet 6 and Violet 7 remain behind with the B-29s five miles south of Iwo Jima at an altitude of 18,000ft.

7. At 1005hrs, the twenty-eight P-38s retire, accompanied by the three B-29 escorts.

8. At 1100hrs, sixty-two B-29 Superfortresses of XXI Bomber Command drop 620 tons of bombs on Iwo Jima by radar.

9. At 1200hrs, 102 B-24 Liberators of VII Bomber Command drop 194 tons of bombs on Iwo Jima by radar from 23,000ft.

10. At 1347hrs, Hoover's Cruiser Division Five, comprising heavy cruisers *Chester*, *Pensacola*, *Salt Lake City*, and six escorting destroyers begin a 70-minute shelling of Iwo Jima.

11. The 318th Fighter Group P-38s begin landing back at Saipan at 1355hrs.

A damaged 318th Fighter Group P-38 limps home to Saipan after a raid on Iwo Jima, January 1945. The P-38 was escorting B-24s to Iwo Jima, but is now being escorted on the long, dangerous trip home by the B-24 that took the photograph. (USAAF)

events quickly proved itself a grave disappointment. The B-29s initially followed standard USAAF doctrine, flying high-altitude daylight "precision" bombing raids of specific Japanese industrial targets from the nearly unassailable altitude of 35,000ft. However, over Japan the Americans quickly discovered the heretofore unknown "jet steam." A phenomenon of the barely understood stratosphere, the jet stream is essentially a ferocious "wind river" well above the troposphere. Boasting a speed of up to several hundred miles per hour, the jet stream caused two serious problems. The first issue was that it made the B-29s' supposed pinpoint bombing horribly inaccurate, ruining the strategic goals of the precision bombing campaign. The second problem was that it wrecked the supposed defensive invulnerability of the B-29s. USAAF brass had previously assumed that by flying 350mph at 32,000ft, the B-29s would be above most accurate Japanese anti-aircraft fire, while the flight envelope rendered ground-to-air fighter interception of the B-29s virtually impossible – even if scrambling Japanese fighters could reach 32,000ft they would be virtually out of fuel and easily outrun by the speedy and well-armed B-29s. However, when forced to fly into the powerful jet stream, the B-29s' formations were easily broken up and their ground speed over the target reduced drastically, allowing Japanese fighters sufficient time to climb to the B-29s' altitude and attack.

The game-changing introduction of the superb P-51 Mustang to Northwest Europe as a Very Long Range bomber escort had long inspired the USAAF's plans to provide the B-29s with similar escort over Japan. However, the abject failure of the early Marianas-based B-29 missions by the XXI Bomber Command made the P-51s' introduction to the missions more vital than ever. Yet even the P-51s lacked the superlative range of the B-29s, meaning that fighter escort of B-29s would have to be provided by captured island bases closer to the Home Islands than the Mariana Islands themselves. For this reason, the VII Fighter Command, suitably re-equipped with P-51D Mustang fighters, was slated to redeploy to Iwo Jima as soon as possible. Eventual plans were for 222 P-51D Mustangs of the VII Fighter Command's 15th and 21st Fighter Groups to redeploy to a captured Iwo Jima. They would be assisted by 24 P-61 Black Widow night fighters of the 548th and 549th Night Fighter Squadrons, which would provide the captured Iwo Jima airfields nighttime interception capability against the Japanese favorite late 1944/early 1945 aerial counterattack tactic, the night heckler and intruder missions. With Iwo Jima slated to become a major USAAF base, it would be crucial that its seaborne logistics be protected by dedicated aircraft. Therefore, in addition to the VII Fighter Command's 222 P-51Ds and 24 P-61s, another 18 TBM Avengers of the

Battleship *Indiana* (BB-58) shells Iwo Jima during a combined-arms bombardment of the island, January 23, 1945. The photograph is taken from a Seventh Air Force B-24 shortly after its own aerial bombing. The Seventh Air Force and the US fleet coordinated several air-sea raids against Iwo Jima between December 1944 and January 1945. (USAAF)

US Marine Corps' VMTB-242 squadron would also deploy to Iwo Jima, where they would defend the VII Fighter Command's logistical lifeline by serving in the maritime patrol and anti-submarine warfare role.

From September 1944, VII Fighter Command commander Brigadier-General Ernest "Mickey" Moore left the Pacific for England, spending two months familiarizing himself with Eighth Air Force P-51 escort operations over Germany. In December 1944, shortly after Moore's return, VII Fighter Command began receiving its first P-51D Mustangs. Flown from Iwo Jima, the long-ranged P-51s would allow the 15th, 21st, and 506th Fighter Groups to escort B-29 raids against the Japanese Home Islands. The three groups would shortly nickname themselves "The Tokyo Club." A period of familiarization followed for the pilots and the ground crews.

On February 2, 1945, the escort carrier USS *Sitkoh Bay* departed Pearl Harbor with all 82 P-51Ds of the 15th Fighter Group aboard, as well as the 15th Fighter Group's pilots. Escort carrier USS *Hollandia* followed a week later with the 21st Fighter Group's P-51s and pilots. The Groups' ground echelons followed aboard Liberty ships. The destination was Guam, where the P-51s were unloaded from the escort carriers by crane. On February 14 the 15th Fighter Group flew its P-51s from Guam to Saipan, followed a week later by the 21st Fighter Group transferring to Tinian.

Between August 10, 1944 and February 15, 1945, US forces had expended 9,616 tons of ordnance on Iwo Jima, including 5,582 tons by VII Bomber Command B-24s. Such profligate bombardment would prove to have been almost completely useless against Iwo's 23,000 extremely well dug-in Japanese troops.

The Seventh Air Force would begin Operation *Detachment* with the 30th Bomb Group operating from Saipan (two fields) and the 11th Bomb Group from Guam; the 494th Bomb Group continued operating under Fifth Air Force from Angaur (Palau Group).

Iwo Jima would be the Seventh's primary target throughout *Detachment*, although nearby Chichi Jima, in the Bonins, would also be consistently attacked. All other Japanese bases in the Central Pacific had been neutralized by this time; even Truk would require only 119 tons of bombs to keep it ineffective throughout the Iwo Jima campaign.

Once again, it was Spruance's Fifth Fleet that would be tasked with capturing Iwo Jima. Operation *Detachment* commenced on February 16, 1945, with three full days of shelling and bombing scheduled. On D-Day, February 19, the US V Amphibious Corps began landing

Seventh Air Force B-24s dump gasoline on Iwo Jima to burn off vegetation, February 1, 1945. By D-Day, February 19, 1945, US air and sea forces would hammer 19,523 tons of munitions onto the miserable little isle, to little substantial effect. (NARA)

its 1st and 2nd Marine Divisions on the miserable black volcanic sand of Iwo Jima, where the marines were expected to pry the Japanese out of their fortified, subterranean defenses in just three days.

Nominally defending the Volcano Islands area was the IJNAF 3rd Air Fleet, comprising 400 operational aircraft. Of these, the Nampo Islands Air Group comprised just six fighters and four bombers based at Iwo Jima and three seaplanes at Chichi Jima. However, IGHQ chose not to waste its hoarded air assets on Iwo Jima. Consequently, only 40 Japanese aircraft would engage the Americans during *Detachment*, but this would include 24 kamikazes.

On D-Day the ground echelons of the 15th Fighter Group floated offshore observing the air-sea bombardment aboard transports *Berrien* and *Lenawee*. They were expected to go ashore and begin readying Iwo Jima's Motoyama No. 1 airstrip for landing the Group's P-51s as soon as practicable. However, the immediate job of preparing the airstrip for American operations fell to vanguard units of Commander R.C. Johnson's 9th Naval Construction (Seabee) Brigade, comprised of the 8th and 41st Naval Construction Regiments and the USAAF's 811th Engineer Aviation Battalion. These engineers hit the beach with the marines on D-Day.

The extremely fierce resistance of the Japanese defenders meant it was not possible to land the 15th Group's ground personnel until February 24, five days after the landings and three days after the entire island had been scheduled to be secure. On that day the 9th Seabee Brigade began crawling across the airstrip, while still under Japanese artillery fire, and removing debris. On the beach, 15th Group was immediately forced to dig foxholes in the black volcanic sand, unable to move. The fighting continued to rage all night, with the USN destroyers offshore continuously firing star shells to prevent Japanese infantry from infiltrating US lines. The ground personnel remained dug in for a full week before they were finally able to leave the beach and reach Motoyama No. 1, which the Americans promptly renamed South Field.

On March 6, the 15th Fighter Group's 47th Fighter Squadron and 548th Night Fighter Squadron departed Saipan and landed at Iwo Jima's South Field, the first echelon in an eventual transfer of the 15th, 21st, and 506th Fighter Groups from the Marianas to Iwo Jima. The following day, March 7, the 15th Fighter Group and 548th Night Fighter Squadron began round-the-clock CAPs over Iwo Jima.

Although the P-51s had been deployed to Iwo Jima with the ultimate intent of escorting B-29 raids to Japan, so long as the ground battle for Iwo Jima raged, the P-51s' only offensive task would be to help secure Iwo Jima. This meant two primary missions: close air support of the marines fighting tooth-and-nail to secure the island, and near-daily neutralization raids against Japanese airbases on outlying islands.

On March 7 the 15th Fighter Group P-51s began flying their first CAS missions in support of the marines. The P-51s had never expected to fly CAS, nor trained for it. But they threw themselves into the CAS mission with significant courage, dedication, and eventual skill. The 15th Group's CAS missions always began with a flight of P-51s taking off from South Field still typically under Japanese artillery or mortar attack. The P-51s would fly a mere few hundred yards past the end of their runway before they were over Japanese

P-51Ds of the 15th Fighter Group fly over Saipan on their way to Iwo Jima, March 7, 1945. They are led by VII Fighter Command skipper Brigadier-General Ernest "Mickey" Moore. Iwo Jima would ultimately host 225 P-51D Mustangs in three separate Fighter Groups. (National World War II Museum)

lines and awaiting CAS calls from marines below. Within a week, Japanese territory had shrunk to the point that friendly fire had become too great a threat. The last CAS mission was flown on March 14.

The P-51s were also expected to suppress enemy airbases. Early on March 11, 15th Fighter Group commander Colonel Jim Beckwith took off from Iwo Jima's South Field with 17 P-51Ds of the 47th Fighter Squadron. Each P-51 was loaded with two 500lb bombs. The primary target was the airfield on the Japanese-held island of Chichi Jima. Along to observe in his own P-51 was the VII Fighter Command skipper, Brigadier-General Moore. Already airborne was a single PBY Catalina, assigned for potential air-sea rescue of downed airmen.

Chichi Jima was defended by 17,000 troops and fortified with anti-aircraft guns, but the Mustangs achieved tactical surprise and dove on the enemy airfield from 10,000ft. The first 12 P-51s dropped their bombs from 4,000ft, and destroyed at least four Japanese aircraft before pulling out in a strafing run over the island. Japanese anti-aircraft guns opened fire at an altitude of 2,000ft. The first echelons of P-51s had caused so much damage and created so much smoke that the last four P-51s aborted the airfield attack and dropped their bombs in Chichi Jima's harbor, apparently causing negligible damage among the Japanese craft anchored there. Beckwith then led his P-51s south towards the Japanese-held island of Haha Jima, strafing the town of Kitmura, along with a weather station and warehouse nearby. Two P-51s had been damaged in the March 11 raid, but none shot down. The successful Chichi Jima raid would be the first in near-daily P-51 strikes against Bonin Islands airfields.

The morning of March 26 brought arguably the biggest shock of the war for the Seventh Air Force, when 350 Japanese troops launched a last-ditch banzai charge against Iwo Jima's US-occupied Central Field. A hodgepodge collection of stunned American rear-echelon troops, including engineers, menial laborers, and VII Fighter Command personnel rallied to repel the assault, grabbing whatever weapons they could find to laboriously re-take each tent and foxhole through hand-to-hand combat.

Some 272 Japanese troops were ultimately hunted down and killed, with only 18 taken prisoner. The banzai charge proved the last organized Japanese resistance on Iwo Jima, but had claimed 53 American dead and 119 wounded; of these the USAAF had suffered 44 killed and nearly 100 wounded. Although the 21st Fighter Group and 549th Night Fighter Squadron had lost a combined 20 men dead and 50 injured in the morning ground action

OPPOSITE TARGETS HIT BY SEVENTH AIR FORCE FROM OKINAWA

(including 11 P-51 pilots as casualties), they nevertheless mounted their usual CAP, with several P-51s flown by wounded pilots. Meanwhile, even as the battle for Central Field raged, the 15th Fighter Group had launched from its own South Field on a morning Chichi Jima sweep, with several concerned pilots noticing the smoke coming from the 21st Group's bivouac. Over Chichi Jima the 15th Group would suffer its first campaign casualty, losing a P-51 and its pilot to anti-aircraft fire. Meanwhile, on March 29, 1945, the P-61s of Iwo Jima's 548th Night Fighter Squadron commenced nightly heckler missions against Bonin Islands airfields.

Operation *Detachment* had cost a staggering 22,114 American casualties, including 5,519 killed and missing. Most had been marines, but VII Fighter Command had suffered 29 dead in the air and on the ground. Between January 1 and March 31, 1945, Seventh Air Force units had flown 3,256 sorties and dropped 5,670 tons of ordnance, including 28 minelaying sorties over Chichi Jima. Of these, the detached 494th Bomb Group, based in the Palaus under V Bomber Command, had dropped 2,168 tons of bombs in 1,187 sorties. Only three Seventh Air Force planes had been lost over Iwo Jima, but 118 had been damaged.

The Ryukyus operation, April–June 1945

The objective of Operation *Iceberg* was the conquest and development of a major base – Okinawa – from which air attacks could be made on the Japanese Home Islands, and an amphibious landing planned and mounted. To accomplish this, Spruance's Fifth Fleet would land Lieutenant-General Simon Buckner's US Tenth Army at Okinawa on L-Day, April 1, 1945.

The initial air support and air defense of the Okinawa invasion would be by USN carrier airpower. However, a new ground-based, joint-branch air force, Major-General Francis C. Mulcahy's (USMC) Tenth Army Tactical Air Force (TAF), was slated for the Ryukyus as soon as Japanese airfields were captured. TAF's fighter force would comprise the Seventh Air Force's 301st Fighter Wing (the 318th, 413th, and 507th Fighter Groups), the 549th Night Fighter Squadron, and – lying outside USAAF operational control – four USMC fighter groups totaling 12 FG Corsair and three F6F Hellcat fighter squadrons.

TAF's bombers fell under VII Bomber Command, whose assets would ultimately include the 11th and 494th Heavy Bombardment Groups (based in the Marianas and Palau, respectively) totaling eight B-24 squadrons; the 41st Medium Bombardment Group (four squadrons); the 319th Light Bombardment Group (four squadrons); two USMC anti-submarine squadrons of TBMs; and the USAAF's 28th Photographic Reconnaissance Squadron.

A Marine observer plane flies over the flattened ruins of Naha, May 1945. The amount of firepower brought to bear on this island over the course of three months would become almost unbelievable. (USMC)

Okinawa's two major airfields, Kadena and Yontan, lay barely a mile inland from the US invasion beaches. Once Kadena and Yontan were captured, the land-based strength of the TAF would be deployed there as fast as possible to provide combat air patrols, close air support, and to hopefully relieve the vulnerable carriers. The TAF's vanguard would be the four USMC fighter groups. TAF's assigned Seventh Air Force contingent would be transferred to Okinawa as soon as circumstances allowed.

However successful American strategy had been thus far, its methodical operational pattern was by now easily predictable to the Japanese high command (IGHQ). By March 1945 the Japanese had massed 3,000 aircraft in four separate air forces to throw at the expected Okinawa invasion: Vice Admiral Matome Ugaki's Fifth Air Fleet; Vice Admiral Kinpei Teraoka's Third Air Fleet; Vice Admiral Minoru Maeda's Tenth Air Fleet; and Lieutenant-General Michio Sugahara's Sixth Air Army. They would be flying from hundreds of bases throughout Honshu and ringing the East China Sea. Indeed, Okinawa was surrounded by Japanese airfields on Kyushu (55 airfields), Formosa (65 airfields), and the Chinese coast. All were within 400 miles, with many closer.

In contrast, heavy Japanese resistance and significant operational delays meant the Seventh Air Force would not gain a foothold on Okinawa until mid-May, some six weeks after the initial landings. Meanwhile, even as *Iceberg* raged, the Seventh Air Force, flying from the Marianas, continued its ongoing neutralization missions against bypassed Japanese airfields. These included Truk, Marcus, Woleai, Pagan, Minami Jima, and Kita Jima.

Spruance's Fifth Fleet once again brought overbearing power to bear on its objective. Off Okinawa, Mitscher's TF-58 now comprised 17 fast carriers; 1,213 carrier aircraft; eight fast battleships; 22 cruisers; and 86 destroyers. Subordinated within Turner's Joint Expeditionary Force (TF-51) were four additional Task Forces. These were the Amphibious Support Force (TF-52); the Northern Attack Force (TF-53) carrying III Amphibious Corps; the Gunfire and Covering Force (TF-54); and the Southern Attack Force (TF-55) carrying XXIV Corps. Meanwhile, Fifth Fleet's 18 escort carriers were assigned to TF-52 and brought another 538 carrier planes to the Ryukyus. In addition, the Royal Navy's newly established British Pacific Fleet (TF-57), while not officially under direct US control, would cooperate closely with Spruance's Fifth Fleet during *Iceberg*. The BPF would bring an additional four fast carriers, 244 carrier aircraft, two fast battleships, five cruisers, and 11 destroyers to the East China Sea, where they would suppress Sakishima Gunto and Formosa airfields on the Americans' western flank. Including the British Pacific Fleet, by L-Day, Fifth Fleet wielded 1,995 single-engine carrier aircraft aboard 21 fast carriers and 18 escort carriers.

Battleship *Tennessee* bombards Okinawa on L-Day, April 1, 1945. An LVT loaded with troops cruises towards the Hagushi landing beaches. As at Iwo Jima, the initial resistance at water's edge was eerily non-existent. It was only after large amounts of American troops came ashore that the Japanese revealed themselves. (Getty Images 588649446)

On March 25, 1945, Spruance's Fifth Fleet commenced the initial air-sea pre-invasion bombardment of Okinawa. Then on April 1 – L-Day – Fifth Fleet landed the III Amphibious Corps and XXIV Corps on western Okinawa virtually without opposition. Within hours the Americans had captured both Kadena and Yontan airfields. However, US aviation engineers found that both had been lightly surfaced and heavily damaged. Yontan had been nearly obliterated by the naval bombardment, but frantic grading work allowed the first USMC fighter groups to base there by April 7. Kadena required extensive crushed coral to properly surface, but the first strip was made dry-weather operational in two days. Constantly bombed, shelled, and strafed, Kadena would not be all-weather operational until May 1.

Despite the initially easy L-Day landings, it quickly became apparent the Japanese troops had merely dug in, and they soon put up a ferocious defense that would persist throughout the months-long ground battle. Then on April 6, Japanese air forces unleashed its first *Kikisui* (mass kamikaze attack) against Fifth Fleet. Most of the 699 Japanese planes were slaughtered, but some inevitably leaked through to inflict serious damage to the US fleet. In addition to individual conventional and kamikaze raids, the Japanese would mount nine more *Kikisui* mass kamikaze attacks against the US fleet into June, although attrition meant each was inevitably smaller and weaker than the previous *Kikisui*.

Although the bulk of Seventh Air Force action now revolved around Okinawa, Iwo Jima, and Japan, the old suppression mission against bypassed Japanese garrisons continued in the rear. The normal dull, predictable pattern of these raids was broken on April 27, 1945, when a USN photoreconnaissance flight observed an Emily flying boat at Truk's Dublon seaplane base, suggesting possible air attacks against the Marianas. Truk had been hit only very intermittently since November 22, and so, in something of an emergency, Hale scrambled to pre-emptively attack Truk while scraping together multiple fighter detachments en route to Okinawa to function in defense. Within seven hours of the USN warning, the 11th Bomb Group was winging its way towards Truk. The Seventh's B-24s and P-47s would hammer Truk daily for two weeks. Thereafter Truk suppression raids fell off to their previously low levels and remained there for the rest of the war.

US anti-aircraft guns erupt against a nighttime Japanese air raid at Yontan airfield, Okinawa, April 16, 1944. With Okinawa surrounded by hundreds of functioning Japanese airfields in close proximity, US fighters, ground-control radars, and searchlights would get a nightly work-out for many months. (Getty Images 615307946)

Destroyer USS *Isherwood* (DD-520) off Ie Shima, mid-April 1945. Ie Shima was a miserable little volcanic rock so small and close to Okinawa that it was within easy sight of the larger island. The Japanese sold Ie Shima dearly, but the little isle would make a fine fighter base for striking Japan. (NHHC 80-G-K-4732)

Meanwhile, back on April 21 the US 77th Division had secured Ie Shima, a volcanic isle just off northwest Okinawa, losing 172 US troops killed. Engineers would restore Ie Shima's airstrip to operational status on April 30, with an all-weather strip ready by May 12. On May 13, P-47Ns of the 318th Fighter Group made their way from Saipan to Ie Shima. The next day they began flying Dumbo escort missions and radar picket CAPs over the American fleet, the first Seventh Air Force sorties staged from Okinawa. However, until a great strength of USAAF airpower could get permanently operational ashore, Mitscher's Fast Carrier Task Force would be forced to remain almost stationary off Okinawa, a sitting duck for mass kamikaze attacks from the scores of surrounding Japanese airfields.

Unfortunately for the Americans, heavy rains began in mid-May, forcing all Okinawa airfield construction to be suspended for several weeks as engineers struggled simply to keep the roads open to Tenth Army. To USN eyes, however, the USAAF engineers ashore required an inordinately long time to get a sufficient number of American airbases up and running. Interservice tension mounted, with USN officers increasingly embittered and suspicious. According to one anecdote, a Fifth Fleet staff officer went ashore touring Okinawa's developing USAAF airfields when he somehow discovered that USAAF chief General Henry "Hap" Arnold had secretly been writing to Okinawa's lead USAAF engineer and urging him to direct assigned fighter strip resources elsewhere to build heavy bomber bases for the Twentieth Air Force to bomb Japan. Incredulous, Spruance stormed ashore to discover if the rumor was true. Stunned, Spruance "got that situation turned around in about 15 minutes."

The night of May 17, two P-47Ns staged a night heckler attack against Kyushu. Shortly afterwards, the 318th Fighter Group was finally unleashed to launch pre-emptive day fighter sweeps against Kyushu. The P-47Ns' two fighter sweeps on May 25 and May 28 combined to claim nearly 40 Japanese air-to-air kills. In addition to fighter sweeps, the P-47s would also fly bombing, rocketing, and strafing missions against targets in the Amami and Sakishima Guntos, the Chusan archipelago, southern Kyushu, and the Chinese coast. These missions were in preparation for the next phase of operations: the air war against the Japanese homeland.

Not all Japanese raids could be stopped. Just after midnight, May 25, Yontan lookouts spotted five Ki-21 Sally bombers approaching. Four fell to US flak, but the fifth Sally survived to crash-land at Yontan airstrip. The flaming Sally immediately expelled ten heavily armed IJA commandos, who promptly began throwing grenades and incendiaries at the parked rows of US aircraft. Operation *Giretsu* – what was left of it – had arrived on schedule. Wild nighttime chaos followed as the IJA commandos sowed wild carnage and destruction, forcing US troops to chase them down. By noon US troops had finally killed all ten *Giretsu* commandos. In the process the Japanese troops had destroyed nine US aircraft, damaged 29 more, and wiped out 70,000 gallons of avgas. The Americans had suffered two killed and 18 wounded, mostly to confused friendly fire. Although not the utter disaster it could have been, the *Giretsu* attack was an embarrassing episode for US airfield defense.

On May 27, Admiral Bill Halsey relieved Spruance in overall command of *Iceberg*. This was a scheduled move and not a reaction to *Iceberg*'s slow progress. Fifth Fleet was now re-designated Third Fleet but remained the same formation.

After weeks of rain, airfield construction resumed in early June, when engineers got two more all-weather strips operational at Ie Shima, along with cramped parking for over 450 aircraft. Following shortly behind the 318th Group in June would be the 507th and 413th Fighter Groups, bringing Ie Shima air strength up to 225 P-47Ns. This belated reinforcement of shore-based airpower allowed Third Fleet's battered fast carriers to finally depart Okinawa on June 10, after 89 straight days on station.

The last organized resistance on Okinawa was finally crushed on June 21. Allied forces had suffered 49,246 total casualties during *Iceberg*, including 12,605 dead. The Americans officially counted 107,539 Japanese military dead on Okinawa, compared to 7,455 captured. When combining estimates of civilian losses, military bodies never recovered, and air-sea actions, total Japanese-Okinawan fatalities approach 180,000. The Japanese had flown roughly 6,000 sorties during *Iceberg*, losing over 4,000 aircraft. About 2,000 of these were kamikazes.

Wreckage of an IJAAF Ki-21 Sally the morning after the *Giretsu* operation. This obsolescent bomber had been modified for special attack duty against US Okinawan airfields in May 1945. One suspects that had any more survived they would have done major damage. The Japanese planned further *Giretsu* operations that were much larger right to the end of the war. (NARA)

B-24 Liberators of the 431st Heavy Bombardment Squadron in the Marianas, June 6 1945. The B-24s in the Marianas continued to hammer Okinawa as well as any bypassed Japanese bases within range. Once the situation at Okinawa settled down, they would be re-deployed to Okinawa to target Kyushu. (Public Domain)

Allied forces had suffered 12,605 total fatalities during *Iceberg*. Japanese suicide attacks had dealt the USN staggering losses off Okinawa, including 36 ships sunk, 368 ships damaged, and nearly 6,000 sailors killed. USN losses at sea were at least partly due to the USAAF's inability to build airfields fast enough or to more successfully defend the fleet. However, in the latter they shared responsibility with the hundreds of USMC and USN fighters who had also failed to better defend the fleet against the formidable kamikaze attacks.

The Seventh Air Force had continued to evolve during the final month of *Iceberg*. Among the developments was a new commander, Brigadier-General Thomas D. White, who assumed command of Seventh Air Force in June 1945.

Reinforcements continued to pour in. On June 16 the 548th Night Fighter Squadron arrived at Ie Shima from Iwo Jima and assumed Kyushu night heckler duty from the 318th Group, whose ill-equipped P-47Ns had been flying them since May 17. Six days later, on June 22, the 494th Bomb Group was finally transferred back to Seventh Air Force and began redeploying at Okinawa.

By June 30, 1945, total TAF strength exceeded 750 planes. During *Iceberg*, VII Fighter Command P-47s and P-61s had flown 1,759 sorties in fighter sweeps and escort missions, while Seventh Air Force strikes had dropped 2,161 tons of bombs in 1,307 sorties. After 18 months of island hopping, the conquest of Okinawa and Ie Shima finally gave the Seventh Air Force its base from which Japan itself could be attacked.

The first Empire missions, April–June 1945

Overarching USAAF strategy in the Pacific War was ultimately dominated by the Boeing B-29 Superfortress. From its introduction in 1944, it was the world's most advanced strategic bomber. The B-29's range, payload, altitude, and speed at altitude were all a quantum leap over previous strategic bombers. Indeed, it was the B-29's extreme range that would allow it to strike Tokyo from the Mariana Islands.

The USAAF controlled its prized Twentieth Air Force directly from Washington, DC. The Twentieth's most prized asset was the XXI Bomber Command, the B-29 bomber force slated for the Marianas. However, fighter escort for the B-29s would require the services of P-51s. The Twentieth Air Force, with its forward XXI Bomber Command headquarters at

Saipan, thus appropriated operational control of the VII Fighter Command at Iwo Jima. As far as top USAAF brass were concerned, XXI Bomber Command was the war's decisive weapon and the Seventh Air Force's three VLR P-51D fighter groups, based in Iwo Jima, would be its handmaidens.

Although the P-51D was technically capable of flying from Iwo Jima to Japan and back, such long-range flights over the featureless and monotonous ocean in single-engine fighters had never been attempted before. The flight profile would be daunting. P-51s would be fully loaded with fuel when they took off from Iwo Jima. They would then have to fly 650nm north over the open ocean, often through severe monsoon conditions before they arrived over heavily defended targets in mainland Japan. They would then have to protect the B-29s by attacking any airborne enemy fighters they discovered. In later missions they would largely be freed from escorting the B-29s and would be sent to strafe any available ground targets in Japan. The return flight was back over 650 miles of featureless ocean, with home being their tiny island of Iwo Jima. At the end of the eight-hour flight the physically exhausted pilots would usually have to be lifted out of their cockpit by their ground crews.

Additionally, because the B-29s were flying from the Marianas and the P-51s from Iwo Jima, the P-51s would have to make a running rendezvous with the B-29s before approaching Japan. Although the P-51s had simple navigation equipment fitted, they were typically shepherded to the rendezvous by a designated B-29 escort that handled much of the fighters' navigation. Finally, the spring season would bring heavy typhoon weather. Fortunately, many pilots in the 15th and 21st Groups had previous combat experience in other theaters, including Northwest Europe. Although the 506th Group would have few combat-experienced fighter pilots when it deployed to Iwo Jima, they all had received extensive training and hundreds of hours' flight experience. Finally, for a training dress rehearsal, on March 30, 1945, the Iwo Jima-based 15th and 21st Fighter Groups flew a practice mission escorting B-29s to Saipan and back. The 1,500nm distance was similar to a round-trip flight from Iwo Jima to the Home Islands.

Ultimately, Brigadier-General Ernest "Mickey" Moore's VII Fighter Command would deploy three P-51 Groups at Iwo Jima, totaling 225 P-51D Mustangs.

Facing the Americans in mainland Japan was Major-General Kanetoshi Kondo's IJAAF 10th Hiko Shidan (Air Division) which defended the Tokyo area. Almost coterminous with Kondo's command was Vice Admiral Kinpei Teraoka's IJN Third Air Fleet, which defended central and eastern Honshu from its own Kanto (Tokyo) district headquarters. Meanwhile the 11th Hiko Shidan defended the Inland Sea area while the 12th Hiko Shidan defended Kyushu. They were partly overlapped by Vice Admiral Matome Ugaki's Fifth Air Fleet, which covered Kyushu and the East China Sea. The potential for mission overlap and redundancy was obvious. On July 9, 1945, operational control of the 11th, 12th, and 13th Hiko Shidan was stripped from their respective district-based Area Armies and consolidated within the unified control of General Masakazu Kawabe's Koku Sogun (Air General Army). Together these formations could marshal 450 fighters in April 1945 and 535 by August. Average flight time by Japanese pilots

P-51D taking off from Iwo Jima, 1945. Veterans of Northwest Europe observed that Japanese fighters and pilot training seemed to be of much lower quality than their German counterparts. When under aerial attack, German pilots knew to dive into range of the Luftwaffe's formidable 88mm anti-aircraft guns, a threat eerily absent over Japan. It was additionally noted that Japanese fighters, lacking self-sealing tanks, caught fire and exploded much easier than Bf 109s. (USAF)

A B-29 crewman views escorting P-51s on a Japan mission, 1945. The B-29 crews were naturally cheered to be accompanied to Japan by the P-51s. But the operational issues involved for the single-engine, single-man P-51s provided a danger difficult for B-29 crews to fully recognize. (USAF)

was just 100 hours; American fighter pilots had four or five times this.

On April 7, 1945, some 108 P-51s of the 15th and 21st Fighter Groups departed Iwo Jima on the first ever "Empire" mission. The P-51s were tasked with escorting 107 B-29s of the 73rd Bomb Wing to the huge Nakajima aircraft engine factory on the western outskirts of Tokyo. Three B-29s were lost, and just one to aerial interception. In turn the P-51s claimed 21 enemy fighters shot down, losing two Mustangs and one pilot. Overall the April 7 escort mission had been a resounding success. The second VLR escort mission was mounted on April 12 and would escort the 73rd Bomb Wing back to Tokyo. The P-51s claimed 15 aerial kills for the loss of four of their own.

On April 16 a last-minute change from a Tokyo escort mission led to a fighter sweep over Kyushu airfields to suppress kamikazes. This mission was plagued by poor weather that precluded damage estimates. This was followed three days later on April 19 by a fighter sweep against the huge Atsugi Naval airfield outside Tokyo. Two P-51s were lost, including one pilot killed and the second becoming the first Tokyo Club member to be taken prisoner. Then on April 22 the P-51s conducted a fighter sweep against the Suzuka airfield in the Nagoya area. During these second and third fighter sweeps the P-51s claimed a combined 32 Japanese planes destroyed in the air and another 30 on the ground.

Four days later, on April 26, poor weather kept the P-51s from finding their B-29s en route to Kanoya and claimed six P-51 pilots. The next B-29 escort mission was against the Tachikawa Army Air Arsenal on April 30. During the month of April, 14 B-29s had been shot down on unescorted missions, but not a single B-29 was lost to enemy fighters when escorted. Nevertheless, the coordination and navigation required to rendezvous with the B-29s was proving difficult, particularly with the seasonally bad weather. The P-51s were already proving themselves more effective at independent fighter sweeps, which ultimately proved a more efficient defense of the B-29s simply by destroying Japanese airpower on the ground.

During each VLR mission, five Air-Sea Rescue (ASR) stations would be set up along the P-51s' route. The first and busiest was the Rally Point just off the Japanese coast. Here the B-29 navigational escort orbited above a surfaced lifeguard submarine and a Superdumbo, escorted by four P-51s. The second station a hundred miles further comprised another submarine/Superdumbo combination, while the third station had a third submarine. The fourth and fifth ASR stations comprised two destroyers each.

The brand-new 506th Fighter Group finally arrived in theater on May 15. Three full P-51 groups were now deployed at Iwo Jima for the VLR campaign against Japan. Three days later the 506th flew its first mission, a desultory raid against Chichi Jima by the 462nd Fighter Squadron. On May 28 the 506th Group mounted its first VLR mission of the war, a fighter sweep against Kasumigaura airfield northeast of Tokyo.

The following day, May 29, was a huge VLR escort mission against Yokohama. As the strike approached Yokohama a total of 150 Japanese fighters scrambled and engaged the Americans. The resulting 650-plane aerial melee may have been the largest single air battle of the war. The P-51s acquitted themselves well, claiming 27 confirmed aerial kills, eight probables, and 23 damaged. However, seven B-29s had been lost to fighters and flak, while another 175 sustained damage, many carrying wounded crewmen on the long flight home.

A P-51 crash on Iwo Jima, June 1945. Operational losses of aircraft far exceeded those shot down by Japanese means. The stress of flying 700 miles out over an empty ocean, engaging in 15 minutes of lethal kill-or-be-killed combat, followed by flying 700 miles back over the same featureless ocean, all while choking down the previous adrenalin, tended to demand much out of pilots. (USAF)

On June 1 the XXI Bomber Command dispatched 450 B-29s to Osaka. For the first time ever, VII Fighter Command deployed all three VLR Groups, sending along 170 P-51s as fighter escort. Unfortunately, severe thunderstorms decimated the escorting P-51s in a disaster forever remembered as "Black Friday." The violent weather wrecked the entire escort formation, as P-51s were forced to turn back, or spun into the sea, or simply disappeared into the stormy murk, never to be seen again. Only 27 P-51s reached Honshu, but no Japanese braved the weather to intercept them. Eleven P-51s of the 45th Squadron settled for opportunistic strafing runs before heading home. Ultimately, 27 P-51s and their pilots had been lost at sea on June 1. Only three pilots were recovered. Among those permanently lost were two groups' mission leaders.

The next VLR mission was June 7, when 138 P-51s from all three groups escorted a B-29 mission to Osaka. Only two Japanese planes were shot down, but the bombing proved effective. June 8 and 9 saw back-to-back fighter sweeps against airfields in the Nagoya area. Only three more escort missions would be flown the rest of the month – June 10 to Tokyo, June 15 to Osaka, and June 26 to Nagoya and Kobe. By now B-29 tactics has begun to evolve and USAAF commanders began to realize the P-51s were more useful hitting airfields. The P-51s accordingly made four more VLR fighter strikes on June 11, June 19, June 23, and June 27, the last two hitting airfields in the Tokyo area.

Endgame over the Empire, July–August 1945

The US capture of Okinawa was a decisive development in the Pacific War. First, Okinawa finally converged Nimitz's Central Pacific drive and MacArthur's South-West Pacific drive into a single location. Secondly, as a large island with several fine anchorages, Okinawa could stage powerful air, land, and sea forces directly against Japan. Third, Pacific War operations had finally become less overwhelmingly naval, as large enemy land masses were now within operational range of significant land-based airpower.

By July 1945 some 245,000 American troops were ashore at Okinawa including 87,000 construction troops building 25 major airfields. The aerial offensive to be mounted from

506th Fighter Group attack Kasumigaura airfield
May 28, 1945

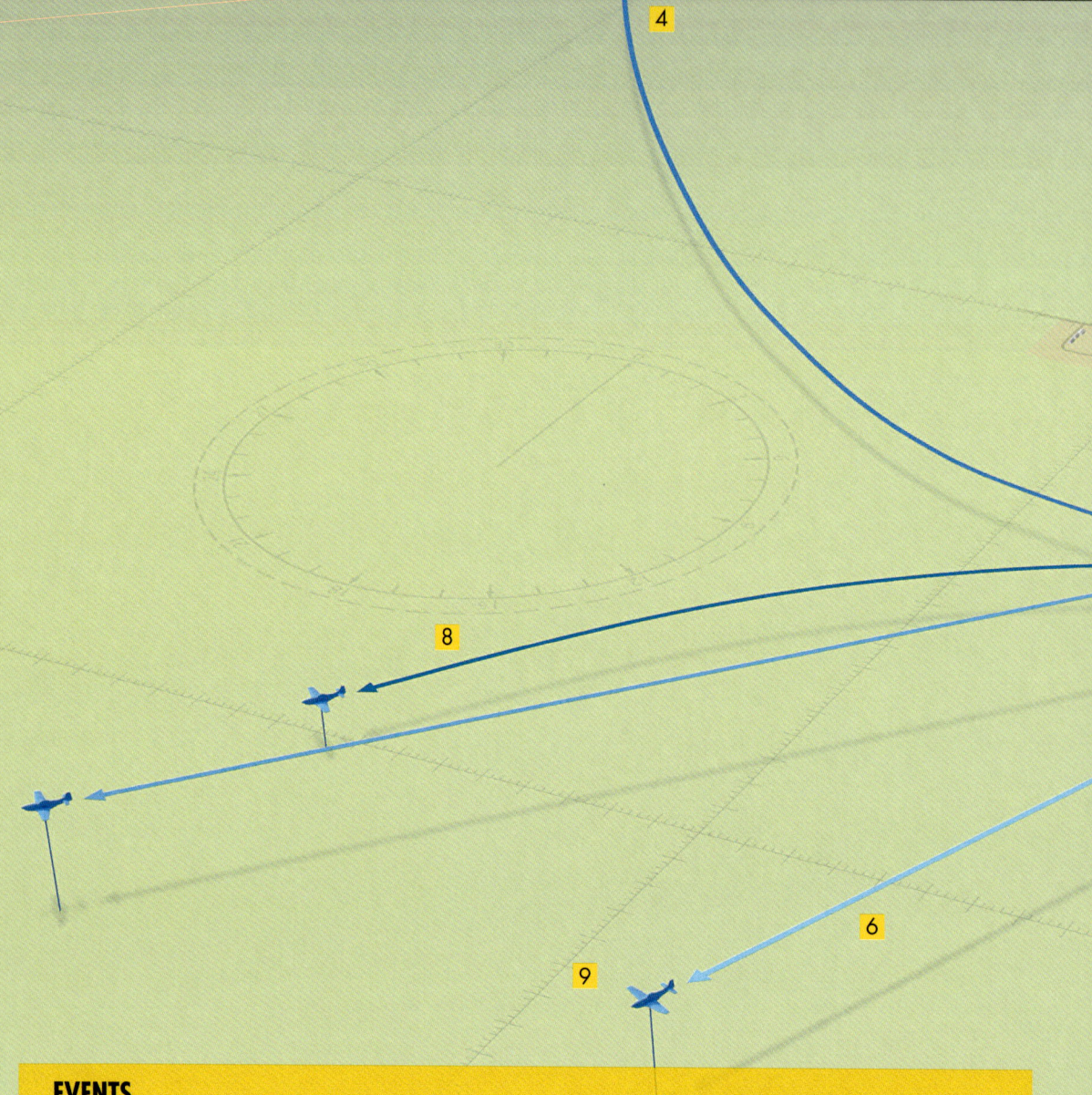

EVENTS

1. Fifty-three P-51D Mustangs of the 506th Fighter Group are airborne from Iwo Jima by 1007hrs.

2. The P-51s rendezvous with the navigator B-29s and are successfully delivered to the DP (Departure Point) at 1340hrs.

3. Led by Colonel Harper, eight Dooley Red Flight P-51s of the 457th Squadron approach from the north-northeast of Kasumigaura airfield at an altitude of 10,000ft. They push over into a 60° dive and strafe Kasumigaura's anti-aircraft batteries before pulling out at an altitude of 4,000ft.

4. Forty-five seconds later, the fourteen P-51s of Major De Jarnette's 462nd Squadron execute a low-altitude strafing run against parked aircraft on the north and south of the airfield as well as the operations center in the middle of the airdrome.

5. Major Watters' eight Dooley Blue Flight P-51s of the 457th Squadron repeat Dooley Red's strafing run against Kasumigaura anti-aircraft defenses.

6. After pulling out of its strafing run, Dooley Blue engages four airborne Japanese fighters, damaging two of them.

KASUMIGAURA AIRFIELD

EVENTS

7. During Dooley Blue's aerial dogfight, sixteen P-51s of Major Shipman's 458th Squadron execute a low-altitude strafing run on parked aircraft, buildings, and a powerhouse. During this pass, the 458th Squadron's Captain Carmody claims the only confirmed aerial kill of the Kasumigaura attack, shooting down a Tojo.

8. Dooley Blue flight circles around and executes a second and final strafing pass against Kasumigaura airfield.

9. The 506th Fighter Group departs Kasumigaura and makes strafing runs against nearby airfields. Among these attacks were Dooley Red leader Colonel Harper strafing Yachimata airfield, while four P-51s of the 462nd Squadron strafed parked aircraft at the secondary target Imba airfield, losing Captain Kensey Miller to a strafing crash. Four P-51s of the 458th Squadron strafe an unidentified airfield, while two P-51s raid Ryugasaki.

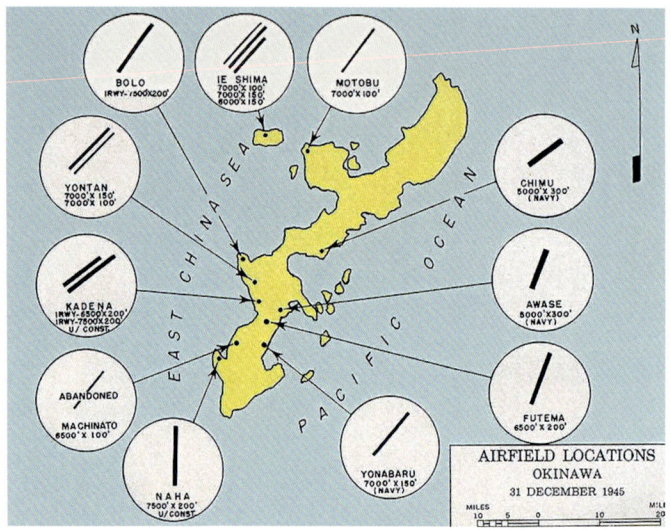

A map of US airfields on Okinawa, December 1945. The sheer number of airfields on Okinawa was expected to fully host the Seventh, Fifth, Thirteenth, and Eighth Air Forces. The Eighth Air Force alone would consist of a staggering 750 B-29s, fully equal to the full power of the XXI Bomber Command flying from the Marianas. (Public Domain)

Okinawa against Japan heralded a new phase in Seventh Air Force operations. Previously, the Seventh had been tasked with the complete neutralization of a few specific Japanese bases, such as Truk or Iwo Jima. By July 1945 the Seventh's attacks would be spread throughout the Japanese Home Islands to interdict 60 highly developed airbases and hundreds of lesser airfields.

Indeed, by midsummer 1945 the Pacific War had entered a new and final phase – the direct assault and defeat of Japan itself. All Allied military power was re-oriented to this goal. Preparations for Operation *Olympic* – the invasion of Kyushu – forced a sweeping theater-wide reorganization of the long sub-optimal command and strategy arrangements in the Pacific theater.

The Fifth Air Force, Seventh Air Force, and Thirteenth Air Force would be assigned to the Far East Air Forces (FEAF), a new umbrella organization that would coordinate all USAAF tactical forces together for Operation *Olympic*. In addition to the Seventh Air Force, the Ryukyus were scheduled to host 29 air groups from the Fifth and Thirteenth Air Forces as well as 750 B-29s from the Eighth Air Force after it was redeployed from Europe. Eleven Ryukyus airstrips were committed to FEAF air groups, including those of the Seventh Air Force.

At Iwo Jima the VII Fighter Command's three P-51 groups were formally put under the operational control of the Twentieth Air Force. The P-51s would continue to fly VLR missions against Japan right to the end of the war, although escort missions had been mostly replaced by fighter sweeps. Between April 7 and August 14, 1945, the Iwo Jima-based P-51 Groups would mount 51 VLR missions against the Home Islands, with poor weather conditions forcing nine of these missions to be aborted before reaching the target. The 15th, 21st, and 506th Groups would fly 140 raids against Bonin Island bases, mostly against Chichi Jima. By the end of the war the Iwo Jima P-51s had shot down a confirmed 234.5 enemy aircraft and destroyed another 219 on the ground. However, total losses for the 15th, 21st, and 506th Fighter Groups would come to 131 P-51s destroyed and 99 pilots killed. Nearly all losses would be due to poor weather and ground fire as opposed to aerial combat.

On July 14, 1945, Tenth Army, Tactical Air Force (TAF) was dissolved and the Seventh Air Force formally transferred from CINCPOA to FEAF, ending the Seventh's three and a half years of operational subordination to USN admirals. Meanwhile the 414th Fighter Group joined the Seventh Air Force in July 1945, the last fighter group to do so. The "Sun Setters" now had 300 P-47Ns of the 318th, 413th, 414th, and 508th Groups operating out of Ie Shima as part of the 301st Fighter Wing. The Seventh finally had all its responsible tactical units based on a single island group, the Ryukyus. Seventh Air Force headquarters, finally back in the operational chain of command thanks to FEAF – began its transfer from the Marianas to Okinawa. The Seventh's only detached air groups – the P-51s of the 15th, 21st, and 506th – remained at Iwo Jima under the operational control of Twentieth Air Force.

Okinawa furnished the base from which light and medium bombers again could reach and hit the Japanese. Deployed at Yontan, Kadena, and Machinato airfields on July 14, 1945 were the B-24s of the 11th and 494th Heavy Bomb Groups, the B-25 Mitchells of the 41st Medium Bomb Group, and the A-26 Invaders of the newly deployed 319th Light Bomb Group. By July 28 the 494th Bomb Group would additionally receive the

P-47N Thunderbolts of the 19th Fighter Squadron, 414th Fighter Group at Okinawa, mid-to-late 1945. The Thunderbolts had spent the past month preparing the Kyushu ground for Operation *Olympic*, just around the corner. (Public Domain)

373rd Bombardment Squadron (Heavy), transferred from the China–Burma–India Theater. The VII Bomber Command's daily operational strength (aircraft ready for combat) during this final offensive would average 93 B-24s, 59 B-25s, and 45 A-26s.

Operation *Olympic* would be preceded and accompanied by an enormous air assault, not only by the Very-Long-Range B-29s from the Marianas escorted by long-range fighters from Iwo Jima and by carrier attacks. From Okinawa would come the full spectrum of USAAF bombers and fighters that would assault the Home Islands from Okinawa, employing high explosives, incendiaries, high and medium altitude attacks, and strafing and rocketing of pinpoint targets from tree-top level. Additionally, the central location of Okinawa's airfields would allow US land-based air to completely dismember Japan's "Greater East Asia Co-Prosperity Sphere" by severing the Empire's shipping lanes with China, Formosa, and Korea.

During this final month of operations the Seventh Air Force reached its peak size and expended maximum effort against the Japanese homeland. As part of FEAF, Seventh Air

P-47N Thunderbolts strafe a train at Tosu, July 6, 1945

It is the summer of 1945, 413th Fighter Group P-47N Thunderbolt fighter-bombers stationed at American-occupied Ie Shima are on a search and destroy mission over Kyushu in the Japanese Home Islands. A section of 413th Fighter Group P-47Ns is seen here strafing a Japanese troop train on Kyushu with rockets and .50cal. machine guns. The Japanese locomotive, a Mitsubishi D51, is leaking steam from several ruptures in its boiler and is either in the process of exploding or will explode very soon from the heavy damage it is taking from the American fighters.

The 413th Fighter Group flew with a distinctive yellow empennage. After arriving in Saipan in late spring 1945, the 413th Group flew several practice strafing missions against Truk in May before deploying to Ie Shima in June. Upon arriving in Ie Shima, the 413th Group immediately began conducting strikes and sweeps of a variety of targets across China and Japan, including factories, radar stations, airfields, small ships, and railyards.

German trains of any importance typically mounted specialized railroad cars of twin or quadruple medium-caliber anti-aircraft guns that fired back at Allied strafers. However, this set-up was apparently less common from the Japanese; in contrast to several flak wagons, this Japanese train only has a single flat car with a pair of 25mm cannon firing back at the P-47Ns.

The 413th had originally been scheduled to be transferred from the Seventh Air Force to the re-deploying Eighth Air Force, where it would help escort the Eighth Air Force's B-29s to Japan. As it happened, by August the Eighth Air Force was not yet operational and the wartime transfer never happened. The 413th Fighter Group P-47Ns flew a single B-29 escort mission on August 8, 1945, escorting XXI Bomber Command B-29s against Yawata. In its only VLR escort mission, the 413th Group scored five confirmed kills and two probables.

Force had three sequential missions. The initial phase was dedicated to destroying Japanese airpower by attacking the dispersal areas of major Japanese airfields on Kyushu. The primary targets were the major enemy airbases at Kanoya, Omura, Tsuiki, and Usa. The second phase of the Seventh's attacks would be to destroy Japanese shipping, but except for a few notable port strikes (such as Kure) relatively little shipping was attacked, largely because not much was left. The final phase of the Seventh Air Force's attacks would be the disruption of transportation and communication systems in Kyushu. This was slated to be the Seventh Air Force's main effort towards the invasion of southern Kyushu (Operation *Olympic*). During this final month the Seventh Air Force would also strike industrial installations and marshalling yards at Nagasaki, Kagoshima, and Tarumizu.

On July 16 the Seventh mounted its first bomber mission from Okinawa, sending A-26s of the 319th (Light) Bomb Group to bomb Miyazaki Airdrome on the east coast of Kyushu. Over the next four weeks the 319th's A-26s would fly 698 sorties on 22 strike missions, delivering 742 tons of bombs against airfields, railyards, shipping, and general industrial targets at Shanghai, the Ryukyu Islands, Kyushu, Chusan, and Nagasaki.

On June 30 Seventh Air Force P-47s had begun the first of four shipping sweeps against the Chusan archipelago, losing three Thunderbolts to destroyer fire. Then on July 22 the 41st Bomb Group's B-25s raided a convoy at the mouth of the Yangtze. The B-25s also experimented unsuccessfully with newly developed glide torpedoes.

Early on July 24, Halsey's Fast Carrier Task Force, now designated TF-38, commenced a huge and controversial series of strikes against Kure to permanently annihilate the immobilized IJN Combined Fleet. However, Kure boasted the densest concentration of anti-aircraft guns in the world and would ultimately claim a heavy 101 USN planes and 88 airmen. Nevertheless, over the course of July 24–28, 16 American and four British fast carriers would fling 4,292 sorties at Kure and the surrounding area in three days of strikes, sinking or heavily damaging three battleships, three fleet carriers, three auxiliary carriers, eight cruisers, six destroyers, three destroyer-escorts, four submarines, one transport, four oilers, and 94 smaller vessels. However, on the last day of the strikes, July 28, the VII Bomber Command inexplicably crashed Halsey's party. From Okinawa, 79 B-24 Liberators of the 11th and 494th Bomb Groups staged a day-long raid against Kure, attacking simultaneously with TF-38's strikes but not planned or coordinated with them. Kure's extraordinary heavy flak claimed two B-24s and damaged 14. For their efforts the B-24s achieved a grand total of four 500lb bomb hits against the already-sunk cruiser *Aoba*, ripping off her stern. Of known USN and USAAF airmen taken captive on July 24–28 at least 12 were imprisoned at nearby Hiroshima and would die in the August 6 atomic bombing.

A-26 Invaders of the 319th (Light) Bomb Group first arrived in Okinawa from the United States in July 1945 and launched their first strike mission on July 16, against an enemy airdrome. Over the final month of hostilities the Invaders would fly 698 sorties on 22 strike missions, delivering 742 tons of bombs against transportation and industrial targets across Kyushu, the Ryukyus, and China. (Public Domain)

The Seventh also engaged in the anti-transportation mission. Between July 17 and August 6, the Seventh Air Force flew 211 sorties against the Kyushu city of Kagoshima, dumping 325 tons of bombs and 15,840 gallons of napalm on its crucial port and rail facilities. On July 16 and July 29, Seventh Air Force B-24s would bomb the vital railroad bridge at Nobeoka, before P-47s of the 318th virtually wrecked it on August 11. The Seventh would also destroy the road bridge at Miyazaki.

The Seventh Air Force's primary industrial target was the city of Nagasaki, a city of 280,000 which, until August 9, had been reserved largely for the Seventh Air Force. Nagasaki's four most important industries were: shipbuilding; ordnance (including torpedoes); steel; and fish canning. All the Seventh's attacks against Nagasaki were concentrated into a single four-day period between July 29 and August 1. The first strike was made by 32 A-26s on July 29. Two days later, on July 31, the Seventh mounted a strike of 29 B-24s. Then on August 1, some 24 B-24s and 26 B-25s hit Nagasaki. The three days of Seventh Air Force raids over the July 29–August 1 period severely damaged the Mitsubishi Steel Works and the Mitsubishi Dockyard and Engine Works. The Mitsubishi Dockyard and Engine Works had been producing two 3,000-ton cargo ships and one 10,400-ton tanker per month; it had also been assigned production of five-man midget submarines. The August 1 raids caused production to drop to zero. One-fourth of Mitsubishi's labor force did not appear for two days after the attack, while later estimates were that six months of repair would have been required to resume 90 percent production.

On August 5 the Seventh and Fifth Air Forces combined in a major raid against a purported suicide rocket plane factory at Tarumizu. Over 300 planes of nearly every type collaborated to drench the area in high explosives and napalm. Two days later on August 7 the P-47Ns of the 318th Group dive-bombed a chemical plant in Kyushu, while the 15th and 506th Groups' P-51s once again found themselves over Tokyo. That same day, P-47s covered 23 B-24s of the 11th Bomb Group when they raided the Mitsui Coal Liquefaction Plant at Omuta, Japan's largest and a producer of 60-octane gasoline, knocking it out of action for seven weeks and reducing the output of nearby coalfields by 500,000 tons.

On August 8 the 414th Fighter Group struck Shikoku while the P-51s of the 21st Group made a return visit to Hanshin airdrome at Osaka. That same day, P-47s of the Ie Shima-based 413th Fighter Group flew their only escort mission of the war, accompanying B-29s in a strike against Yawata. Then on August 10 a Seventh Air Force raid of similar type to the Tarumizu raid set Kumamoto ablaze; the following day 53 Seventh Air Force B-24s burned down over one-fourth of the city of Kurume. Seventh Air Force operations were suspended the following day, August 12, as rumors of a Japanese surrender broke out. Offensive sorties were resumed the morning of August 14 but were shortly aborted as word came of the Japanese government's surrender.

Between July 1 and August 14, VII Bomber Command (B-24s, B-25s, and A-26s) had flown 3,055 effective sorties and dropped 4,840 tons of ordnance against 76 total targets in Japan, China, and the Ryukyus. Of these, 54 targets had been in the Home Islands, mostly on Kyushu. Ten targets in China were attacked, all in Shanghai or the Chusan area. The final 12 targets were mostly in the Ryukyus. These were largely airfields, but shipping, transportation, and industrial targets were also struck. Many Seventh Air Force planes, especially B-25s of the 41st Bomb Group, had flown two missions per day during the final days of the war.

AFTERMATH AND ANALYSIS
Success in the islands

B-25s of the 41st Bombardment Group at Okinawa, summer 1945. The B-25s are preparing the ground for Operation *Olympic*. They will be striking trains, roads, and coastwise shipping. Fortunately, partly due to the Seventh Air Force's efforts, the apocalyptic call to execute *Olympic* never comes. (USAF)

The Seventh Air Force greatly expanded its operating area throughout the war. When war broke out, the Seventh's main airbases were on Oahu, although landing strips were available at Midway, Canton, and Christmas Atolls. Only in 1943 were additional airfields constructed on Baker Island and in the Ellice Group (Funafuti, Nukufetau, and Nanomea). The successful conclusion of *Galvanic* allowed the construction of airfields in the Gilberts (Tarawa, Makin, and Abemama) by December 1943. Three months later, in March 1944, the Seventh Air Force was able to add Kwajalein and Eniwetok in the Marshalls. By July the Seventh was operating out of the Marianas before adding multiple airfields on Iwo Jima and the Ryukyus in March and May 1945.

During the 1943–45 Central Pacific offensive, the Seventh Air Force flew over 26,000 sorties and dropped more than 30,000 tons of ordnance on Japanese targets. The Seventh Air Force attacked the widest array of targets of any air force of the war. These included targets in the Gilbert, Marshall, Caroline, Mariana, Bonin, Volcano, Ryukyu, and Home Islands – in short halfway across the Pacific and a fourth of the way across the globe. Its combat sorties comprised some of the longest of the war (thousands of miles) as well as the shortest (hundreds of yards).

The Seventh contributed air strikes in support of amphibious landings, including the Gilberts (Tarawa and Makin), the Marshalls (Kwajalein), the Marianas (Tinian and Guam), and the Volcano Islands (Iwo Jima). While all these operations saw the Seventh engage in pre-invasion bombardment, by the Marianas campaign Seventh Air Force fighters and medium bombers were also participating in on-call close air support.

The success of the island-hopping strategy meant the Seventh was also forced to engage in the long-term neutralization of Japanese airfields. Because the Japanese were unable to supply or reinforce bypassed islands, the garrisons here were unable to realize any offensive power and effectively left to "whither on the vine." The greatest proof of this is the Americans' ability to concentrate large numbers of airplanes wingtip-to-wingtip on islands like Kwajalein and Saipan. The Seventh Air Force also directly eliminated Japanese aircraft, claiming 336 aerial kills and another 122 destroyed on the ground. Never were the Japanese able to maintain any great strength at airbases within range of the Seventh Air Force.

Conversely the Seventh Air Force successfully defended the United States' own bases. Although occasional harassing raids were made, the Japanese were never able to mount a sustained air offensive against US airbases, even though the limited size of the Americans' island airfields made aircraft dispersal impractical. The Seventh Air Force also conducted aerial reconnaissance of Japanese shipping lanes, airfields, and island garrisons. The Ellice, Gilbert, Marshall and Mariana Islands were all reconnoitered by the Seventh Air Force, while visual and photographic reconnaissance was continually made of bypassed Japanese bases. Finally, the Seventh also engaged, to a lesser degree, in attacks on Japanese shipping, and in the strategic bombing of industrial targets on the Home Islands, particularly Kyushu.

The Seventh Air Force was never large, nor was it ever the primary player in any theater. However it was the USAAF's main contribution to the Central Pacific island-hopping campaign. By 1945 the Seventh Air Force was arguably the most diverse Air Force the USAAF had ever fielded in terms of missions, aircraft, equipment, and geographic deployment.

SELECT BIBLIOGRAPHY

Arakaki, Leatrice, and Kuborn, John R. (1991). *7 December 1941: The Air Force Story.* Pacific Air Forces – Office of History. Hickam Air Force Base, Hawaii.

Buell, Thomas B. (1974). *The Quiet Warrior: A Biography of Admiral Raymond A. Spruance.* Little, Brown. Boston.

Cate, James Lee and Craven, Wesley Frank (eds) (1983). *The Army Air Forces in World War II, Vol. V. The Pacific: Matterhorn to Nagasaki June 1944 to August 1945.* Office of Air Force History.

Cate, James Lee and Craven, Wesley Frank (eds.) (1950). *The Army Air Forces in World War II, Vol. IV. The Pacific: Guadalcanal to Saipan August 1942 to July 1944.* Office of Air Force History.

Dorr, Robert F. (1999). *B-24 Liberator Units of the Pacific War.* Osprey Publishing.

Ellis, Maj Peter S. H. (2002). *Hale's Handful … Up from the Ashes: The Forging of the Seventh Air Force from the Ashes of Pearl Harbor to the Triumph of VJ-Day.* Air University Press.

Herder, Brian Lane (2023). *Early Pacific Raids 1942: The American Carriers Strike Back.* Osprey Publishing.

Herder, Brian Lane (2022). *East China Sea 1945: Climax of the Kamikaze.* Osprey Publishing.

Herder, Brian Lane (2020). *The Naval Siege of Japan 1945: War Plan Orange Triumphant.* Osprey Publishing.

Herder, Brian Lane (2019). *World War II US Fast Carrier Task Force Tactics.* Osprey Publishing.

Howard, Clive and Whitley, Joe (1946). *One Damned Island After Another.* University of North Carolina Press.

Lambert, John W. (1990). *The Pineapple Air Force: Pearl Harbor to Tokyo.* Phalanx Publishing.

Masterson, Bud (1988). *AAF: The Official World War II Guide to the Army Air Forces.* Bonanza Books; Crown Publisher Inc. New York. New York.

McFarland, Steven (1998). *Conquering the Night: Army Air Forces Night Fighters at War.* Air Force History and Museums Program.

Melson, Maj. Charles D. (1996). *Condition Red: Marine Defense Battalions in World War II.* History and Museums Division, Headquarters, U.S. Marine Corps. Washington, DC.

Military Analysis Division (1947). *The United States Strategic Bombing Survey: The Seventh and Eleventh Air Forces in the War against Japan.* U.S. Strategic Bombing Survey (Pacific) Naval Analysis Division. Washington.

Military Analysis Division (1946). *The United States Strategic Bombing Survey: The Campaigns of the Pacific War.* U.S. Strategic Bombing Survey (Pacific) Naval Analysis Division. Washington.

Molesworth, Carl (2006). *Very Long Range P-51 Mustang Units of the Pacific War.* Osprey Publishing.

Morison, Samuel E. (2001). *Victory in the Pacific 1945.* Castle Books.

Rottman, Gordon L. (2004). *The Marshall Islands 1944: Operation Flintlock, the capture of Kwajalein and Eniwetok.* Osprey Publishing.

Rottman, Gordon L. (2004). *US Marine Corps Pacific Theater of Operations 1941–43.* Osprey Publishing.

Rottman, Gordon L. (2003). *Japanese Pacific Island Defenses 1941–45.* Osprey Publishing.

Rottman, Gordon L. (2002). *World War II Pacific Island Guide: A Geo-Military Study.* Greenwood Press. Westport, CT.

Schaefer, Daniel J. (2024). *The Beaming Sun: The Effectiveness of Imperial Japanese Radar against United States Aircraft during the Battle for Saipan.*

Stanaway, John (1999). *Mustang and Thunderbolt Aces of the Pacific and CBI.* Osprey Publishing.

War Department (1944). *Technical Manual: Handbook on Japanese Military Forces. 15 September 1944.*

Williamson, Dr. Corbin (2021). "Expeditionary Airfields in the Pacific, 1941–1945" in *Wild Blue Yonder* online journal.

Wright, Derrick (2000). *Tarawa 1943: The turning of the tide.* Osprey Publishing.

Zaloga, Steven (2010). *Defense of Japan 1945.* Osprey Publishing.

https://ibiblio.org/hyperwar
https://www.navsource.org/
https://pacificwrecks.com/
http://pwencycl.kgbudge.com/
https://www.7thaf.org/
https://www.7thfighter.com

INDEX

Note: page numbers in **bold** refer to illustrations, captions and plates.

7th Weather Squadron, Army Air Force 14
XXI Bomber Command 63, 66–70, 80–81, 83, 86–87

"Acorn" airbase type 13, 43
Air Service Support Squadrons (ASSRONS) 40
aircraft
  American
    fighters, Very Long Range (VLR) 17–18
      see also North American P-51 Mustang; Republic P-47N Thunderbolt
    Bell P-39 Airacobra 5, **11**, 17, **50**
    Boeing B-17 Flying Fortress **6**
    Boeing B-29 Superfortress 24, **65**, 66–72, 81
    Consolidated B-24 Liberator 5, 14–16, **16**, **36**, **49**, **52–53** (51), 67, 72, **80**
    Consolidated LB-30 Liberator 67
    Consolidated PBY Catalina 24, **25**
    Curtiss P-40 Warhawk 5, 16, 17, **31**, **44**
    Douglas A-24 Banshee 5, 18, **46**
    Douglas A-26 Invader 5, 20, **90**
    Douglas P-70 Nighthawk 5, 22, **22**
    Goodyear FG Corsair 5
    Grumman F6F Hellcat 5
    Lockheed P-38 Lightning 5, 17, **70**
    Martin B-26 Marauder 6
    North American B-25 Mitchell 5, 18, **20**, **62**, **92**
    North American P-51 Mustang 4, 5, 17–18, 70–71, **73**, 81, **81**, **82**, **83**
    Northrop P-61 Black Widow 5, 22, **60–61** (59), 64
    Republic P-47 Thunderbolt 4, **4**, 5, **17**, 17–18, **23**, 35, 58, 66, **87**, **88–89** (87)
  Japanese 28–30
    Kawanishi H8K Emily **26**, 29, 40
    Kawanishi N1K Shiden Kai/George 30
    Kawasaki Ki-45 Nick 30
    Kawasaki Ki-61 Tony 30, **30**

    Mitsubishi A6M Zero 17, 28
    Mitsubishi G4M Betty 29, 40–42
    Mitsubishi Ki-21 Sally 29, **79**
    Nakajima J1N1 Gekko/Irving **28**, 28–29
    Nakajima Ki-44 Tojo 30
Angaur Island, Palau 64
armament 14, 16, 17, 18, 20
Army Air Forces, Pacific Ocean Areas (AAFPOA) 14, 63
artillery, Japanese anti-aircraft **27**, 27–28
Aslito Field, Saipan 56, 58, 63
Atsugi Naval Airfield, Tokyo 82

Baker Island 14, 37, 39–40
banzai charge, Iwo Jima 73
Beckwith, Colonel Jim 73
Betio Island 37, 41–42, **43**, **62**
"Black Friday" 83
Buckner, Lieutenant-General Simon 74

Canton Island 32, 35, 37, 44
Caroline Islands 26, 48–49, **50**–55
  see also under individual islands
carrier operations 22–24
Catchpole, Operation 42, 48–49
Chichi Jima 71, 73
close air support (CAS) 72–73
Conolly, Rear Admiral Richard L. 47, 62
coral construction material 13

defense battalions, USMC 20–21
defenses, Japanese 27–30, 40
Detachment, Operation 67, 71–74
Douglas Jr, Brigadier-General Robert W. 32, 55
"Dumbo" (SAR) aircraft 24–25
  see also Search and Rescue

early warning, Japanese 29
East Field, Saipan **66**
Ellice Islands **15**
  see also under individual islands
Emmons, Lieutenant-General Delos C. 12
Eniwetok Atoll **13**, 49

Fifth Fleet 58, 71, 74–79
firebombs 62
Flintlock, Operation 42–47

Forager, Operation 56–62
Fort Shafter, Hawaii 12
fuel, bulk systems 14
Funafuti Island 35, 37

Galvanic, Operation 36–42
gasoline bombs **72**
Gilbert Islands 7, **15**, 35–42
  see also under individual islands
Giretsu, Operation **79**, 79
Granite II, Campaign Plan 55–56
Guam 26, 56, 62–63

Hale, Major-General Willis H. 12, **12**, 36, 55
Halsey, Admiral Bill 79
Hansell, Major-General Haywood 67
Harmon, Lieutenant-General Millard F. 63, **63**
Hawaiian Air Depot 34
Hawkins Field, Betio Island 43, **62**
Henderson, Second Lieutenant Herb 49
Hickam Field, Hawaii 5, **6**
Hill, Rear Admiral Harry W. 37
Home Islands, attacks on Japanese 83–90
Hoover, Vice Admiral John H. **8**, 12

Iceberg, Operation 67, 74–80
Ie Shima Island 78, **78**, 79
Isley Field, Saipan 64, **65**
  see also Aslito Field, Saipan
Iwo Jima 4, **21**, 63–77, **68–69**

Jaluit Atoll 37, 41, 42, 46
jet stream, high altitude 70
Johnston Island 6

kamikaze 72, 77
Kasumigaura Airfield, Tokyo 82, **84–85**
Kawabe, General Masakazu 81
Kobayashi, Vice Admiral Masami 26, **27**
Kobler Field, Saipan 64
Kondo, Major-General Kanetoshi 81
Kure 90
Kurume 91
Kusaie airbase 43, 48
Kwajalein Atoll 42–44, **47**, 47–48
Kyushu Island 78, 86

Landon, Major-General Truman 47
Luzon Island 67

INDEX

MacArthur, General Douglas 11
Maeda, Vice Admiral Minoru 76
Majuro Atoll 42
Makin Island 18, 36, 37, 41–44, **46**
Maloelap airbase 36, 42, 46
Marine Corps, US 9, 20, 31–32, 37–38, 43, 56–57, 74, 80
Marshall Islands **15**, 42–50
  see also under individual islands
Marston matting 13–14, 39
Merritt, Brigadier-General L.G. 37
Midway Atoll 6, 34
Mili Island 46–48
Mille Island 37, 41, 42
Mitscher, Vice Admiral Marc 47, 56
Moore, Brigadier-General Ernest "Mickey" **48**, 49, 71, 73, 81
Mulcahy, Major-General Francis C. 74
Mullinix Field, Buota Island 43

Nagasaki 11, 91
Nagumo, Vice Admiral Chuichi 56
Nampo Shoto island chain 63–64
Nanomea Island 31, 37, 39–40, **40**
Nauru Island 7, **36**
Naval Construction Battalions (Seabees) 13, 37, 43, **43**
night fighting 21–22
Nimitz, Admiral Chester 11, **12**
Nukufetau Island 37, 39

Obata, Lieutenant-General Hideyoshi 56
O'Hare Field, Apamama Island 43
Okinawa Island 67, 74–80, 83–84, **86**
Olympic, Operation 4, 86
Omuta 91
Osaka 83

Pacific Fleet, British 76
Pearl Harbor 5
"Pineapple Air Force" *see* Seventh Air Force
Ponape airbase 43, 48
Pownall, Vice Admiral Baldy 37

radar
  airborne 21–22, **22**
  ground 21, **21**
  Japanese 27, 29
radio nets 59
Reed, Brigadier-General Walter 34
Roi airbase 37, 42–43
Ryukyus operation 74–80

Saipan, Northern Mariana Islands 56–59, **60–61** (59), 73
  see also under individual airfields
Saito, Lieutenant-General Yoshitsugu 56
Seabees *see* Naval Construction Battalions (Seabees)
Search and Rescue 24–25, 44, 46, 78, 82
Seventh Air Force
  command 11–12
  originally Hawaiian Air Force 4, **5**
  patch **5**
  5th Pursuit Wing *see* VII Fighter Command
  18th Bombardment Wing *see* VII Bomber Command
  VII Bomber Command 6, 12, 36–37, 54–55, 65
    11th Bomb Group 35–40, 54–55, 63, 71–74, 81, 90–91
    30th Bomb Group 37–38, 54, 63, 65, 71
    41st (Medium) Bomb Group 18, 37, 43, 46, 54, 62, 65, 72–74, 90–92
    319th (Light) Bombardment Group 20, 74, 86, 90
  VII Fighter Command 4–10, 18, 32, 46–50, 63, 70–74, 80–83
    15th Fighter Group 49–50, 70–74, 81–82, 86, 91
    21st Fighter Group 17, 49–50, 70–74, 81–82, 86, 91
    318th Fighter Group 17, 56–58, 62–70, 78–80, 91
    413th Fighter Group 74, 79, 86–87, **88–89** (87), 91
    414th Fighter Group 17, **23**, 86–87, 91
    508th Fighter Group 86
  VII Service Command 34
  19th Troop Carrier Squadron 38
Shikoku 91
ships
  American
    fast carriers **9**, 22–23, **23**, **31**, 39, 54
    Breton, USS 44, **44**
    Chester, USS 66–67
    Curtiss, USS 40, **41**
    Hancock, USS **9**
    Hollandia, USS 71
    Hornet, USS **9**
    Independence, USS 42
    Indiana, USS **70**

Isherwood, USS **78**
Manila Bay, USS 58, **58**
Maryland, USS 41
Nassau, USS 44
Natoma Bay, USS 58
Pensacola, USS 66–67
Salt Lake City, USS 66–67
Saratoga, USS **31**, 32
Sargent Bay, USS 62
Sitkoh Bay, USS 71
Tennessee, USS **76**
Ticonderoga, USS **9**
Wasp, USS **9**
Yorktown, USS **9**
Japanese
  Akagi 6
  Hiryu **7**
South Field, Iwo Jima 72–73
Spruance, Admiral Raymond 34, **34**, 79
Starmann Field, Makin Island 43, **50**
Sugahara, Lieutenant-General Michio 76
"Sun Setters" *see* Seventh Air Force, VII Fighter Command
surrender, Japanese 91
Suzuka airfield, Nagoya 82

tactics **19** (18), **57** (56)
Tarawa Island 7, 35, 37, 39–41, 43
Taroa Island 46–47
Tarumizu 91
Taylor, Lieutenant-Colonel Charlie 58
Tenth Army Tactical Air Force (TAF) 74, 86
Teraoka, Vice Admiral Kinpei 76, 81
Tinian 58
Tinian Island 56, 58, 62
Tinker, Major-General Clarence L. 5, 7, 12
Truk (Chuuk) Atoll 26, 40, 42, 50–55, **51**, **52–53** (51), 65, 77
Turner, Vice Admiral Richmond K. 37, **37**, 47, 56

Ugaki, Vice Admiral Matome 76, 81

Wake Island 7, 35, **55**
weather services 14
Wheeler Field, Hawaii 5
White, Brigadier-General Thomas D. 80
Wotje Island **42**, 42–43

Yokohama 82
Yontan airfield, Okinawa 74, 77, **77**